COVENTRY CITY
AN ILLUSTRATED HISTORY

DESERT ISLAND FOOTBALL HISTORIES
www.desertislandbooks.com

COVENTRY CITY
AN ILLUSTRATED HISTORY

Series Editor: Clive Leatherdale

JIM BROWN

DESERT ISLAND BOOKS

First Published in 2000

DESERT ISLAND BOOKS

89 Park Street, Westcliff-on-Sea, Essex SS0 7PD

United Kingdom

www.desertislandbooks.com

British Library Cataloguing-in-Publication Data

A catalogue record for this book is available from the British Library

ISBN: 1-874287-36-8

Printed in Great Britain

by

Redwood Books, Trowbridge, Wiltshire

The publishers acknowledge with thanks the following for provision of photographs for this
book: The Coventry Evening Telegraph, Coventry City FC, Edna Davis, Joan Barratt, David
Brassington, Les Wood, Chris Lambert, Barry Ireland, Rod Ison, Rod Metcalf, Tom Partridge
and Bob Hill.

This book was conceived, designed, and produced by
Brand Digital Design
www.branddigitaldesign.co.uk

Chapter 1.

The club was formed in 1883 as Singers Football Club by employees of Singers, the cycle firm who at the time were situated in Alma Street. The club's first headquarters were at the White Lion Hotel, Gosford Green, and the first ground was close to the present Gosford Park Hotel in St Georges Road, and was known as Dowells Field. Over the first four years of the club's existence they played about 40 games, although many of these were of a rudimentary nature. But all that changed in 1887 when J G Morgan became secretary and under his guidance the club was transformed. That same year the club moved to a new ground, Stoke Road, situated a little to the south of King Richard Street, between Walsgrave Road and Lansdowne Street. The ground had an enclosure with a small grandstand and a twopenny admission fee taken at the west side of the ground at the club's headquarters at the Binley Oak in Paynes Lane. The club also had its first fixture list and entered the Birmingham Junior Cup for the first time.

The period of 1887 to 1892 was a golden one for the 'Little Blackbirds' as the club became nicknamed, with the Birmingham Junior Cup being won in consecutive years in 1891 and 1892.

On the back of the Cup success membership of the Birmingham and District League was secured in 1894, and matches were played against the strong reserve sides of Aston Villa, West Brom, Wolves and Small Heath. In August 1898 the club's name was changed to Coventry City FC and a year later the ground at Highfield Road was opened. The first season at the new ground was dismal; the team finished bottom of the league and suffered several heavy defeats. The next few seasons were a depressing period for the club with severe financial difficulties and a conspicuous lack of success on the pitch. In 1907 the club became a limited company with shares being issued and the first board of directors. On the field there were also signs of improvement and in 1907-08 the side had their first FA Cup success, reaching the first round proper for the first time.

In 1908 the FA Cup success resulted in election to the Southern League but their first season was traumatic and only an extension of the league from 20 to 22 clubs enabled them to avoid relegation. The following season they enjoyed one of their finest moments when as a non-league club they reached the FA Cup quarter-finals, beating First Division Preston and Nottingham Forest before losing to Everton.

In 1910-11 another Cup shock saw Sheffield Wednesday defeated on their own ground and in 1912, the Bantams, as they were now nicknamed, lost to First Division Manchester United in the FA Cup but finished sixth in the Southern League, their highest ever position. Poor gates and financial problems hindered the club's progress in the years up to World War I and relegation to Division Two of the Southern League was suffered in 1914. A year later, after an unsatisfactory season, the club closed for the duration of the war.

One of the earliest known pictures of the Singers team taken in April 1891 after the club's first trophy success. They beat Willenhall Pickwicks 1-0 at Aston Villa's ground to lift the Birmingham Junior Cup. Over 2,500 Singers fans travelled to the game, many by train, many by bicycle and the attendance was over 6,000. Frank Mobley's first-half goal sparked wild scenes amongst the Singers fans. Back in Coventry, thousands of fans met the team's train and lined the route from the station to the Queens Head where their president George Singer laid on a banquet.

1891-92 was the last of five great seasons for the football club and three trophies were reward for an excellent campaign. The Birmingham Junior Cup was retained with another victory over Willenhall. The Walsall Cup was clinched with a 3-1 win over Bloxwich Strollers and the Wednesbury Cup was shared with the professionals of Wednesbury Old Athletic after a drawn semi-final game which Singers claimed after Athletic refused to play extra-time. The Wednesbury FA controversially awarded the game to Athletic, only for the more senior Birmingham FA to overrule them after they had won the final. The final decision was a shared trophy.

In 1898 the club changed its name to Coventry City and this is the first team picture taken before a Birmingham League game in their dark and light blue halved shirts. Under their new name they failed to win any of their first six games but recovered to finish 7th in what was their last season at Stoke Road before moving to Highfield Road. There are no details of the players but centre of the back row is goalkeeper Nat Robinson and the player second from the left in the middle row is captain Joe Whitehouse.

COVENTRY CITY FOOTBALL TEAM.
S. Bullivant (Trainer). T. Bolton. J. Kearns. H. Whitehouse. H. King. G. Beale. M. O'Shea (Sec.)
F. Court. E. Clive. H. E. Banks (Capt.) H. Jones. G. Archer.
S. Edwards. W. R. Spittle.

By 1904-05 the club was in a bad financial state and the future was very uncertain. The team photo was taken before an early season home game with Walsall. Harry Whitehouse is recalled in goal after a 1-7 hammering from Aston Villa's reserves the previous week. Bertie Banks has the ball at his feet. The Coventry-born player had returned to the city after a successful career with Millwall, Aston Villa, Bristol City and Watford and was the first international to play for the club, having won one England cap whilst with Millwall in 1901. Team: Back row (left to right): S Bullivant (trainer), T Bolton, J Kearns, H Whitehouse, H King, G Beale, M O'Shea (Secretary). Front row: F Court, E Clive, HE Banks, H Jones, G Archer. Seated on ground: S Edwards, W Spittle.

In 1905 the club's committee was disbanded and a syndicate took over the running of the club. Former player Joe Beaman became manager and Harry Whitehouse captain. Second from right in the front row is James McIntyre, signed from Notts County, who scored a hat-trick on his home debut and ended with 19 goals in 24 games. He later became manager of the club.

COVENTRY CITY FOOTBALL TEAM.

| Beaman, J. | Jones, H. | Edwards, F.J. | H. A. Whitehouse (Capt.) | Gilbert, H. | Smith, E. | Parks, W. |
| O. MAULE & CO. | | Such, E. | Arnold, T. | Kinsey, L. | A. Wright | Tooth, J. G. |

A crowd of around 2,500 is dotted around the banking to see the first home game of 1907 with Wolves Reserves as the visitors. Albert Lewis, the superstar of the era, was absent and it needed a goal from winger John Tooth to salvage a point. With a very settled side, City finished 7th in the Birmingham League. Lewis scored fifty goals in two seasons before the famous Herbert Chapman, then manager of Northampton, tempted him away.

"THE MIDLAND DAILY TELEGRAPH" [Gratis.

OFFICIAL TEAM-SHEET.

English Cup, 1st Round, Coventry City v. Crystal Palace, at Coventry, Jan. 11, 1908.

CRYSTAL PALACE.

(Cardinal and blue jerseys, white knickers.)

RIGHT WING.

JOHNSON.
(1)

LEFT WING.

NEEDHAM.
(2)

WALKER.
(3)

FORSTER.
(4)

RYAN.
(5)

BREARLEY.
(6)

ROBERTS.
(7)

SWANN.
(8)

INNERD.
(9)

WOODGER.
(10)

DAVIES.
(11)

TOOTH.
(12)

LEWIS.
(13)

WARREN.
(14)

SMITH.
(15)

LAYTON.
(16)

CHAPLIN.
(17)

GILBERT.
(18)

JONES.
(19)

KIFFORD.
(20)

JUGGINS.
(21)

H. A. WHITEHOUSE.
(22)

LEFT WING.

RIGHT WING.

COVENTRY CITY.

(Light and dark blue jerseys, white knickers.)

REFEREE: MR. T. KYLES (Aylesbury).   LINESMEN { MR. W. L. PURCELL (Derby).
{ MR. W. BRADSHAW (Coalville).

Any Alteration in the Teams will be shown on a Board.

In 1907-08 City reached the 1st round of the FA Cup for the first time (the equivalent of the 3rd round now) after winning through six qualifying rounds. A ground record crowd of 9,884 saw Southern League Crystal Palace win 4-2. Lewis and teenager Billy Smith were the heroes of the Cup run with fourteen goals between them. The programme is believed to be the earliest known production, a special given out free by the Midland Daily Telegraph.

Prior to the big tie with Crystal Palace, the team went for special training to Droitwich where they took the town's special spa waters. Middle row (left to right): S Bullivant (trainer), J Kifford, Fred Chaplin, Bert Gilbert, John Tooth. Front row: Will Layton, Billy Smith, George Warren, H Jones and W Parkes. Standing behind are E Juggins and R Tipping.

Joe Moult took over in goal from the great Harry Whitehouse and was a regular for two seasons.

Will Layton, a right-winger came from Wolves and played over 60 games in two seasons including the 1907-08 FA Cup run.

Jack Dougherty, a wing-half signed from Birmingham who played a number of games in the first season in the Southern League, 1908-09.

A Archer, a goalkeeper signed from Atherstone in 1908 who made a handful of appearances in 1908-09.

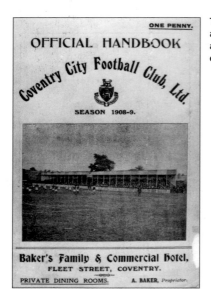

The Highfield Road ground opened in September 1899 and consisted of one stand and three banked sides. The 'John Bull' stand, named after the advertisement that adorned the roof, was built of wood, roofed with corrugated iron, and was coloured chocolate and light blue.

Goalkeeper Bob Evans was signed in 1909 and kept goal for City for four seasons becoming the club's first international when he was selected five times for Wales. He left to join Birmingham in 1913 but returned to work in the Coventry area, later becoming a referee and a senior figure in local football.

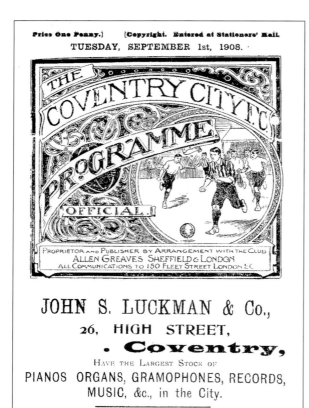

The club were elected to the Southern League in 1908 and their opening game was at home to Crystal Palace on a Tuesday afternoon. 5,000 fans watched the historic game and the club started issuing programmes on a regular basis. The game ended 1-1 but it was the only point gained in the first six games.

Eli Bradley was the outstanding City player of the Southern League era. Although he was a good centre-forward, City played him as a centre-half and his robust style and fierce long-range shooting made him a crowd favourite. He played over 100 games for the club and was the captain and a major influence in the 1910 FA Cup run.

OUR FOOTBALL CARTOON.

LADY GODIVA AT EASTVILLE.

ROVER: Entree, sweet maid! (Aside) Fain would I squelch thee to make a Rovers' holiday!

October 1908. The Bristol Echo portray City as Lady Godiva and Bristol Rovers as a pirate. City upset the cocky Bristolians by ending their poor start to the season by winning 3-1 at Eastville.

August 1909. The team, now nicknamed the Bantams, have their photo call for the new season with optimism high. It was to be the club's most successful season to date with FA Cup wins over First Division sides Preston and Nottingham Forest before losing at the quarter-final stage to Everton, and 8th place achieved in the Southern League. Stalwarts such as Eli Juggins, Harry Buckle, now player-manager, Tubby Warren and Fred Chaplin are joined by new signings Bob Evans from Croydon Common, Eli Bradley from Luton and Billy Smith, returning after a season with Birmingham. Two months into the season the signing of England cricketer Patsy Hendren sparked a run of 19 league and cup games with only three defeats.

R.BARNACLE.   A.NEWBIGGING.

P.SAUL.   R.O.EVANS.

A.CHAPLIN.   W.R.HICKLETON.

February 1910. On the day that City beat Portsmouth at Fratton Park to go through to the 3rd round of the FA Cup, Highfield Road played host to an international trial match in aid of the British Red Cross Society. The prices of stand seats were increased because of the appearance of some of the stars of the day including Jesse Pennington of West Brom, Harry Hampton of Aston Villa and Reverend Kenneth Hunt of Wolves.

The FA Cup giantkillers of 1910. Qualifying round wins at Wrexham (3-0) and Kettering (5-0) earned a plum draw at Preston. Whilst the Deepdale men weren't in the class of the 1888 invincibles, they were expected to win comfortably and City were 20-1 on to win. They won 2-1 and then defeated Portsmouth away 1-0 before a record Highfield Road crowd of 12,500 saw Nottingham Forest humbled 3-1. Over 19,000 crammed into the ground for the quarter-final clash with Everton but the Merseysiders' class won the day, 2-0. Back row (left to right): E Kinnear (trainer), Hickleton, Saul, Evans, Bradley (captain), Hanson, Chaplin; front row: Tickle, Warren, Smith, Hendren, Buckle (player-manager).

April 1912. A third successive FA Cup giantkilling run has been halted by the mighty Manchester United who, inspired by the great Billy Meredith, won 5-1 at Highfield Road. City's cup success is restricted to the Southern Charity Cup where they met Southend in the final at White Hart Lane but lost 0-1 to the Shrimpers who wore salmon and pink striped shirts. In the league a highest ever placing of 6th is achieved.

Billy Yates was signed from Portsmouth and played 102 successive games in the Bantams defence between 1911-14. He was wounded during World War I.

The record receipts from the Everton game enabled the club to build a new stand on the Highfield Road side of the ground. This grandstand was to last 54 years until replaced by the Sky Blue Stand. The trees at the Swan Lane end of the ground are prominent in what was then countryside.

The 1912-13 side are pictured in a fetching light blue kit. The team finished 13th in the Southern League Division 1 and fell at the first hurdle in the FA Cup despite an excellent 1-1 draw at Old Trafford. In the replay 20,042 watched the First Division giants win 2-1.

The club handbook from 1913-14 season shows the club's officials. Although Chairman David Cooke had been a substantial benefactor in earlier years and would be so again in 1917 when the club came close to extinction he refused to bankroll the purchase of new players. As a result the team were relegated in 1914 after failing to win a league match between November and April. Despite being responsible for team affairs, Robert Wallace was named as secretary in the days when the role was a dual one covering administration as well as the playing side.

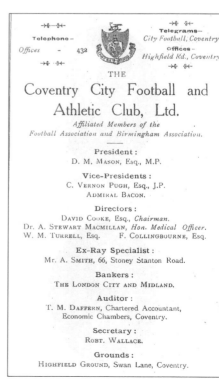

Telephone— Offices - 432

Telegrams— City Football, Coventry Offices - Highfield Rd., Coventry

THE

Coventry City Football and Athletic Club, Ltd.

Affiliated Members of the Football Association and Birmingham Association.

President :
D. M. Mason, Esq., M.P.

Vice-Presidents :
C. Vernon Pugh, Esq., J.P.
Admiral Bacon.

Directors :
David Cooke, Esq., *Chairman.*
Dr. A. Stewart Macmillan, *Hon. Medical Officer.*
W. M. Turrell, Esq.   F. Collingbourne, Esq.

Ex-Ray Specialist :
Mr. A. Smith, 66, Stoney Stanton Road.

Bankers :
The London City and Midland.

Auditor :
T. M. Daffern, Chartered Accountant, Economic Chambers, Coventry.

Secretary :
Robt. Wallace.

Grounds :
Highfield Ground, Swan Lane, Coventry.

COVENTRY CITY FOOTBALL CLUB.

PRICES OF ADMISSION.

GENTLEMEN.

SEASON TICKETS.

Ground only		10/6
„ „ Boys under 16		5/3
„ and Wings, Old Stand		12/6
„ Centre Old Stand		15/-
„ Wings, New „		17/6
„ Centre „ „		25/-

LADIES.

Ground Ticket (admitting lady to any part of Old Stand) ...	10/6
To Ground and Centre of New Stand	15/-
„ „ „ Wings of „ „	12/6

PRICES OF ADMISSION.

SOUTHERN LEAGUE.

To Ground		6d.
New Stand, Centre	extra	1/-
„ „ Wings	„	6d.
Old „ Centre	„	4d.
„ „ Wings	„	2d.

Ladies admitted free to Wings of New Stand and any part of Old Stand. To centre of New Stand a charge of 3d. extra.

BIRMINGHAM LEAGUE.

To Ground		4d.
New Stand, Centre	extra	8d.
„ „ Wings	„	5d.
Old „ any part	„	2d.

Ladies admitted free to Wings of New Stand and any part of Old Stand. To centre of New Stand a charge of 3d. extra.

Admission prices for 1913-14 season. A boys ground season ticket cost 5s 3d (26p) whilst the most expensive season ticket, in the centre of the new stand cost 25/- (£1.25) for a gentleman but only 15/- (75p) for a lady.

The CHELSEA F.C. Chronicle

OFFICIAL PROGRAMME of

Che Chelsea Football & Athletic Company, Limited.

MEMBERS OF

The Football League (Division 1)   South Eastern League (Division 1)

VOL. IX. No. 44   Wednesday, April 1st, 1914   ONE PENNY
POST FREE 11/2d.

COVENTRY CITY v. SOUTHAMPTON

SOUTHERN CHARITY CUP—FINAL

COVENTRY CITY (Dark and Light Blue)

JAQUES
Goal

BEXTER   BARNACLE
Right Back   Left Back

YATES   FEEBURY   TOSSWELL
Right Half   Centre Half   Left Half

CHITTON   DOBSON   DAVISON   JONES   HOLMES
Outside Right   Inside Right   Centre   Inside Left   Outside Left

Kick-off   5.0 p.m.

BLAKE   ANDREWS   HOLLINS   DOMINY   KIMPTON
Outside Left   Inside Left   Centre   Inside Right   Outside Right

McALPINE   DENBY   SMALL
Left Half   Centre Half   Right Half

IRELAND   LEE
Left Back   Right Back

STEVENTON
Goal

SOUTHAMPTON (Red and White Stripes)

Referee - - - Mr. W. R. CHILD

Linesmen - - Messrs. J. LUCAS and B. E. DRAKE

Printed and Published for the Proprietors (The Chelsea Football and Athletic Co., Ltd.), by Jas. Truscott & Son, Ltd., London.

Another Southern Charity Cup final, this time against Southampton at Stamford Bridge. City's wretched league form is forgotten as the Saints, managed by former City player, James McIntyre, are held 2-2 and then beaten 0-1 in the replay at Millwall three weeks later.

Chapter 2.

Having had their debts paid off by benefactor David Cooke in 1917, Coventry City ended the hostilities confident of gaining entry to the Football League and in March 1919 they received the necessary votes and the first official post-war season saw City admitted to Division Two.

City lost the opening game 0-5 at home to Spurs, starting a period of ill-fortune which lasted, with barely any respite, for the next twelve years. The period was known as the 'Stormy period' with five different boards of directors and eight different managers in charge of team affairs. On the field the team successfully fought five successive relegation battles but succumbed in the 1924-25 season. There followed a season in Division Three (North) before a geographical reorganisation saw them switched to the Southern Section, where they continued to struggle apart from a sixth-placed finish in 1930.

The dreadful era came to an end by the end of 1931 with Walter Brandish in charge in the boardroom and his appointee, Harry Storer, as manager.

That first league season was dreadful; it was ten games before they took a point and it took twenty games before they recorded their first victory, over Stoke on Christmas Day. By then, manager William Clayton had resigned, with Harry Pollitt taking over in November. They staged a New Year recovery and avoided having to apply for re-election by winning their last game, against Bury. City were later found guilty of bribing Bury players to lose the vital game and Pollitt, David Cooke and captain George Chaplin were later banned from the game for life.

After two managers in their first season, it was incredible that Albert Evans lasted five years in the job but the team's dire form in 1924-25 rendered his departure inevitable. Scotsman James Kerr took over and proceeded to ship in Scots exiles, many of whom played a handful of games before returning north of the border.

In 1927 Kerr was sacked after another early exit from the FA Cup and Mr A Saunders took over as caretaker. A financial crisis was triggered when a cheque to Notts County for the purchase of Dinsdale and Widdowson bounced. Once again David Cooke came to the rescue, paying off Notts County and securing loans.

James McIntyre arrived as manager in 1928, made some astute signings and by Christmas the team were within a point of the league leaders. They finished tenth but the following season improved to sixth and gave First Division Sunderland a shock in the FA Cup before losing 1-2. Season 1930-31 started full of optimism but a string of poor results, an early Cup exit and interference from the boardroom forced McIntyre to resign, paving the way for the arrival of Harry Storer.

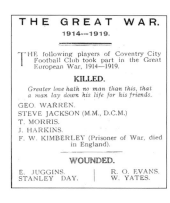

THE GREAT WAR.
1914—1919.

THE following players of Coventry City Football Club took part in the Great European War, 1914—1919.

KILLED.

Greater love hath no man than this, that a man lay down his life for his friends.

GEO. WARREN.
STEVE JACKSON (M.M., D.C.M.)
T. MORRIS.
J. HARKINS.
F. W. KIMBERLEY (Prisoner of War, died in England).

WOUNDED.

E. JUGGINS.	R. O. EVANS.
STANLEY DAY.	W. YATES.

A sombre reminder that several City players were either killed or wounded in the Great War. Most sport ceased with the outbreak of war in 1914, but soccer, fearful of its financial future, carried on. City, along with many other clubs, were criticised for this and it was barely worth the effort. Gates fell to around 2,000 as there was very little interest in opposition drawn mainly from South Wales. After finishing 5th out of 13 clubs in Division Two of the Southern League the club unsuccessfully applied to join the Central League, leaving them with no league, no money and very few players. It was just as well that the government cancelled all sport indefinitely.

David Cooke joined the Coventry City board in 1909. At the time he said: 'What money I possess I have made in Coventry, and if I can do anything to further the interests of Coventry City I feel I should do it.' He had earned his wealth as a local tobacco magnate and in 1891 had introduced the famous 'Three Cups' tobacco in recognition of Singers winning the Birmingham Junior Cup, Coventry Rugby Club winning the Midland Counties Cup and their junior side winning the Junior Cup. His cash injections allowed the club to prosper between 1909-12 and to survive a crisis in 1917 by paying off three years rent-arrears on the ground. Then after election to the Football League in 1919 he provided a further £5,000, an enormous sum in those days, to strengthen the team. In 1922 he cancelled all loans owed to him by the club, the phenomenal sum of £15,400, and left the board to become president after criticism from shareholders. A year later he was banned from any involvement in football following the shameful Bury bribery scandal in 1920.

In 1919 the club were elected to Division Two of the Football League and they kicked off with a home game with Tottenham Hotspur. An outstanding Spurs team, destined to be champions with 70 points, ran rings round City and won 5-0. A week later City travelled to White Hart Lane for the return and in front of 30,000 fans lost 1-4. The programme cover shows that Tottenham's Cocky cockerel is certainly happy with the result of his poaching whilst Coventry's gamekeeper says "If I'd have known he was anything out of the ordinary I'd have seen he was dished out with a few blank cartridges, bust him!"

City, depicted as an elephant (from the City's elephant and castle crest), dream of delivering a knockout blow to Spurs' cockerel. Sadly it wasn't to be.

LEAGUE COLOURS

COVENTRY CITY

B.D.V. CIGARETTES

A cigarette card depicting a Coventry City player from 1919 in the light blue and white striped shirts and white shorts.

THE "WHITE ELEPHANT" OF THE SECOND DIVISION.

COVENTRY CITY

BRISTOL CITY

Bristol City and Coventry City met this afternoon.
Bristol Boy: "Watch me tickle him, and see if he falls over."

October 1919. The cartoon from the Birmingham Sports Argus shows a forlorn elephant about to be tickled by a boy representing Bristol City and implying that victory will be easy. City had only won two points from their first eleven games and duly lost 0-1 at Ashton Gate. It would be Christmas Day before the Bantams registered their first win in the League, a 3-2 home victory over Stoke City. The fans however were loyal with gates averaging over 17,000.

The team photo in January 1920. City used 43 players during the season and manager William Clayton was sacked in October before a game had been won. His successor, Harry Pollitt, was given money to spend on new players and slowly they turned the corner. Four wins out of the last six games guaranteed safety in 20th position. Back row (left to right): H Hobbins, D Cooke (Chairman), H Pollitt (secretary/manager), H Harbourne (Financial secretary), W Fulljames (Trainer), F Crowe. Middle row: H Taylor (Trainer), B Robinson, T Hanney (Captain), R Roberts, A Lindon, A Fenwick, G Chaplin, S Blake (Trainer). Front row: J Dougall, G Wynn, W Walker, F Jones, A Sheldon.

September 1920. The team line-up for the first home game of the new season under a new manager, former Villa player Albert Evans, with only four players from the previous team photograph. It is déjà vu with only one win in the first ten games and an amazing escape act with six wins in the last ten games to avoid relegation. Back row (left to right): S Blake (Trainer), G Wynn, A Fenwick, G Chaplin, J Mitchell, T Hanney, J Lawrence, Hughes (Assistant Trainer), G Hadley, AJ Evans (Team manager). Front row: J Dougall, A Mercer, R Parker, H Nash, F Gibson.

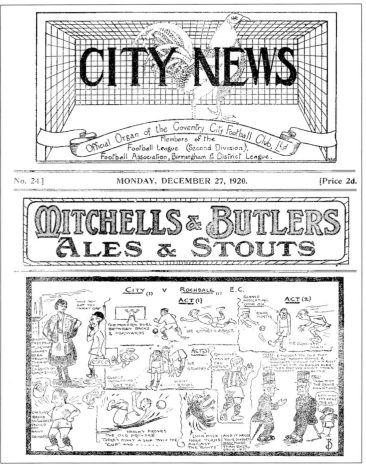

December 1920. The programme cover for a reserve team game with Nuneaton Town tells the story of City's FA Cup exit at non-league Rochdale, a team that would return to haunt them in the 1970s. After being Cup experts in the Edwardian age, it would be 1937 before the club reached the last sixteen as a league club and 1963 before they again graced the quarter-finals.

Danny Shea joined City from Fulham in 1923 and was paid a record £7 a week. The 36-year-old veteran had been capped for England before the war and he played 66 games for City scoring 12 goals in two seasons.

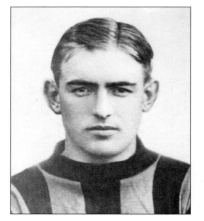

William 'Mollie' Morgan was a left-sided forward who scored 14 goals in 57 games in the relegation battles of 1921 and 1922. He was sold to Crystal Palace in 1922.

Sammy Stevens became the first City player to score 20 goals in a league season in 1921-22. Signed from Notts County for £1,300 and standing only 5 feet 8 inches tall, injury curtailed his career in 1923.

George Chaplin was capped for Scotland before the Great War and joined City in 1918. He was the captain during City's first season in the League and was at the centre of the Bury bribery scandal and was later banned 'sine die'.

Bert Millard was signed from Birmingham in 1920 as a centre-forward but was converted to centre-half at Coventry. He played 68 games in two seasons before joining Crystal Palace. He later kept a pub in Leamington.

Jerry Best was the first of City's great goalkeepers. The Geordie stood only 5 feet 6 inches tall and carried a wartime injury in his arm but made up in courage and agility. He played 236 games between 1920 and 1926.

In five seasons at Highfield Road Coventry-born centre-half Reg Dalton played only 54 games but was a key player in the relegation dog-fights. A knee injury ended his career in 1924.

Jimmy Dougall signed or City as a 19-year-old in 1920 and was a regular on the right wing for seven seasons. Over the years City rejected several offers for him from big clubs, including one of £2,000 from Manchester United. He made 238 appearances for City, then a record, before joining Reading.

Scotsman Billy Leitch was signed from Partick Thistle in 1920 but failed to hold a regular place and left to join Bournemouth in 1923 after 29 games.

Richard Lindley was signed from Bradford City in 1921 as a successful goalscoring inside-forward but failed to impress in 15 games in 1921-22, scoring only once.

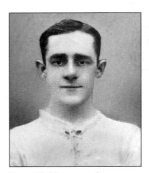

Benny Robinson made 22 appearances in the catastrophic 1919-20 season as a strong half-back. After only eight games in the subsequent two seasons he joined Nuneaton Town.

Signed from Aston Villa in 1920, Jimmy Lawrence was the regular left-back for three seasons, making 134 appearances. He retired through injury in 1925.

In 1922 the club decided to update their image. Out went the traditional blue and white shirts, replaced by green and red halves (Coventry's civic colours) with a large coat of arms prominent on the shirt, while the stands and offices received a new coat of paint to match. The programme for that season reflected the new image with the first colour cover printed in green and red.

The team pictured in their red and green shirts in October 1923. Back row (left to right): N Findlay, G Allon, J Jones, J Best, S Foster, H Richmond, H Lake (Trainer), J Dougall. Front row: J Randle, F MacLachlan, D Shea, E Winship, F Herbert, A Wood. Kneeling: T Storey and J Rowley.

City visited Stamford Bridge on the opening day of 1924-25 season, what would turn out to be a miserable season of relegation to Division Three. Chelsea newly relegated from Division 1 won 1-0.

Jimmy Dougall and Danny Shea in November 1924 back in blue and white shirts. Shea, by this time 36-years old and carrying a lot of weight, had lost his pace but still had a superb football brain.

The programme for 1924-25, somewhat pompously described as 'the official organ' with Mitchell and Butlers the brewers commencing a long and mutually beneficial relationship with the club.

The appointment of James McIntyre as manager in the summer of 1928 saw the club have their best season of the decade and the signs that a troubled period in the history was coming to an end. The Scottish manager's early signings included Billy Lake, a prolific scorer from Walsall, Jimmy Loughlin, another forward who cost £1,300 from West Ham and Tommy 'Shadow' Allen (right), a spectacular goalkeeper who had played over 300 games for Southampton under McIntyre. Allen was to be first-choice keeper for four seasons, playing over 160 games.

Another McIntyre signing was Laurie Crown who hailed from Sunderland and joined City from Bury at the age of 30. The six-footer made the right-back position his own for three seasons and captained the club until his retirement in 1931.

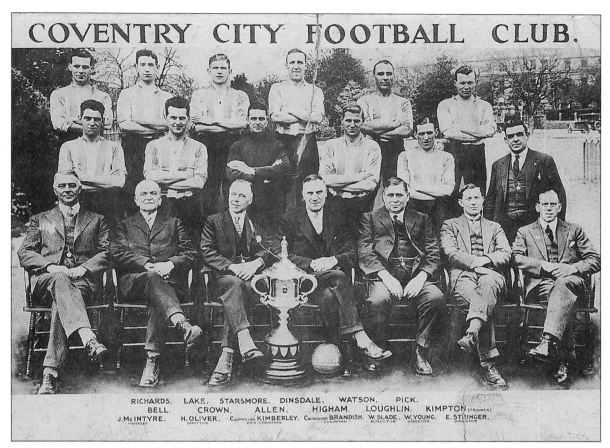

COVENTRY CITY FOOTBALL CLUB.

RICHARDS. LAKE. STARSMORE. DINSDALE. WATSON. PICK.
BELL. CROWN. ALLEN. HIGHAM. LOUGHLIN. KIMPTON (TRAINER)
J. McINTYRE. H. OLIVER. Councillor KIMBERLEY. Councillor BRANDISH. W. SLADE. W. YOUNG. E. STRINGER.
MANAGER DIRECTOR VICE-CHAIRMAN CHAIRMAN DIRECTOR DIRECTOR DIRECTOR

McIntyre's first season saw a rare trophy lifted. In April 1929 City played Birmingham for the Lord Mayors Hospital Charity Cup. The game ended 4-4 but City kept the trophy. A crowd of 3,187 saw the game and City's scorers were Loughlin 2, Pick and Starsmore. The trophy was played for regularly in the 1920s and 1930s and City had lost to Birmingham the previous season but beat Wolves 4-1 in 1931. Back row (left to right): W Richards, W Lake, J Starsmore, N Dinsdale, E Watson, W Pick. Middle row: W Bell, L Crown, T Allen, F Higham, J Loughlin, Kimpton (Trainer). Front row: J McIntyre (Manager), H Oliver (Director), Councillor Kimberley (Vice Chairman), W Brandish (Chairman), W Slade (Director), W Young (Director), E Stringer (Director).

Chapter 3.

The 1930s were the most successful years for Coventry City until the Sky Blue era. Against a backdrop of a prosperous and expanding city - Coventry remained relatively untouched by the economic depression of the 1930s - the football club put the frustrations of the previous decade behind them.

The appointment of Harry Storer as manager in 1931 was the catalyst for change and the new manager's signing of Clarrie Bourton and Jock Lauderdale for a combined fee of £1,000 that summer was a master-stroke. By the end of their first season this famous strike partnership had become the idols of the terraces. Bourton bagged a remarkable 49 goals as City scored 108 overall - they were to score over 100 goals in four out of the next five seasons. The following season Bourton netted 40 goals and the team finished a creditable sixth in Division Three (South).

By 1933-34, City's great team was taking shape and the first real promotion challenge was mounted. With gates averaging over 15,000, the club were able to strengthen the squad by signing Welsh international Leslie Jones. They finished second that season and third in 1934-35 (only one team was promoted in those days). New signings George McNestry, Arthur Fitton and Jack Astley were added to the emerging homegrown talent such as George Mason, Bill Morgan and Billy Frith, not to mention the still potent scorer Bourton. The result was an outstanding team that deservedly won the championship after beating off a strong challenge from Reading and Luton.

The team was strengthened again after promotion and with a greater emphasis on defence the side made a big impression in the higher division. They finished in a creditable eighth position in 1936-37 but had their best Cup run for over 25 years with a record Highfield Road crowd of 44,492 watching the fifth-round tie with West Brom, which the Baggies won 3-2.

There is little doubt that the team should have won promotion in 1937-38. They had a fifteen-game unbeaten start to the season and were never out of the top four despite selling Jones to Arsenal and Bourton, by now a spent force, to Plymouth. In March, with the promotion challenge faltering and injuries to key players, Storer refused to sign the players that could have made promotion certain. City missed out by one point, leaving the fans frustrated and feeling that perhaps the club did not want promotion.

Although they finished fourth again in 1939, it was a fitful season and supporters drifted away with average attendances down by 6,000. In September 1939, with the season only three games old the start of the war meant that all competitive football was suspended and it was never discovered whether City could make it third time lucky in their quest for promotion.

McIntyre remained in charge until February 1931 when he was forced to resign after a string of poor results and gates slipping under 10,000. He said, 'My reasons for resigning are consequent upon the intolerable attitude of Walter Brandish and under no account could I carry on under his Chairmanship'. Brandish set about the task of finding a new manager, sifting his way through a hundred applicants. On 8 April the board announced that Harry Storer (left) had been appointed manager. The former England wing-half was only 33 and had been a first-team regular at Burnley the previous season and was also a talented opening batsman for Derbyshire. His appointment was to signal the start of the golden era for the club.

September 1931. An early home game in the Storer era. Exeter City are humbled 4-0 and new signing Clarrie Bourton scores one of his two goals, with Billy Lake and Frank Bowden also on the scoresheet.

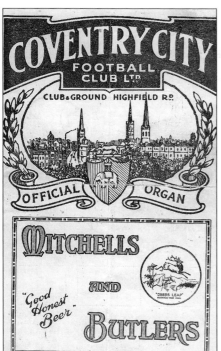

February 1932. The programme for City's game with Crystal Palace and the old rivals from the Southern League are comprehensively beaten 8-0, with Bourton scoring his fifth hat-trick of a memorable season when he finished as the League's leading marksman with 49 goals. In total the Bantams scored 108 goals and would have finished higher than 12th but for a dismal defensive record which saw them concede 97 goals. They scored five or more goals on seven occasions and revived the former nickname of Foleshill Great Heath - 'the Old Five'.

George Mason was signed from Birmingham junior club Redhill Amateurs in 1932 and for three years learned his trade in the reserves, playing the occasional first-team game. He became the regular centre-half in 1934, captain a year later, and was considered to be Storer's lieutenant on the pitch. He went on to play 350 games for the club and but for the war the total would have been over 600. He won international recognition when chosen to play for England in two wartime internationals and finally retired in 1952 at the age of 38.

An Agreement

made the ___Twenty-first___

day of ___April___ 19 33 between ___Harry___

___Storer___ of ___Highfield Road,___

___Coventry___ in the COUNTY OF ___Warwickshire___

the Secretary of and acting pursuant to Resolution and Authority for and on behalf of the ___Coventry City___ FOOTBALL CLUB, of ___Highfield Road, Coventry___ (hereinafter referred to as the Club) of the one part and ___Clarence Frederick Tom Bourton,___

of ___34, Dane Road, Coventry.___

in the County of ___Warwickshire___ Professional Football Player

(hereinafter referred to as the Player) of the other part **Whereby** it is agreed as follows :—

1. The Player hereby agrees to play in an efficient manner and to the best of his ability for the Club.

2. The Player shall attend the Club's ground or any other place decided upon by the Club for the purposes of or in connection with his training as a Player pursuant to the instructions of the Secretary, Manager, or Trainer of the Club, or of such other person, or persons, as the Club may appoint. [This provision shall not apply if the Player is engaged by the Club at a weekly wage of less than One Pound, or at a wage per match.]

3. The Player shall do everything necessary to get and keep himself in the best possible condition so as to render the most efficient service to the Club, and will carry out all the training and other instructions of the Club through its representative officials.

4. The Player shall observe and be subject to all the Rules, Regulations, and Bye-laws of The Football Association, and any other Association, League, or Combination of which the Club shall be a member. And this Agreement shall be subject to any action which shall be taken by The Football Association under their Rules for the suspension or termination of the Football Season, and if any such suspension or termination shall be decided upon, the payment of wages shall likewise be suspended or terminated, as the case may be.

5. The Player shall not engage in any business or live in any place which the Directors (or Committee) of the Club may deem unsuitable.

Clarrie Bourton's contract which shows him to be earning £8 a week (£6 in the summer) with an extra £1 if he was in the first team. Despite having scored 93 goals in the previous two seasons, the Football Association rules precluded him from being paid more than the maximum wage.

ance by the said player of the terms, provisions

said ___H. Storer___

of the Club hereby agrees that the said Club

um of ___£6---------___ per week from

___to 19th August 1933___

from ___21st August 1933___

the Rules of The Football Association)

___May 1934___

viously determined in accordance with the

receive one pound per week extra
st Team, also the usual bonuses
& Combination of which the Club

As Witness the hands of the said parties the day and year first aforesaid.

Signed by the said ___H. Storer___)

and

___C.F.T. Bourton___

In the presence of ___F. Rogers___

(SIGNATURE) ___F Rogers___

(OCCUPATION) ___Clerk___

(ADDRESS) ___Highfield Road,___

___Coventry___

C. F. T. Bourton.

H Storer

In the 1930s every newspaper had its cartoonist drawing caricatures of the footballers of the day. This cartoon appeared in October 1934 after a 5-1 home win over Millwall. City were riding high at the top of the table and promotion to Division 2 looked a good bet but poor away form resulted in them finishing in third place. Promotion, however, was only delayed for twelve months.

A pre-season photograph of the side which would win promotion in 1935-36. They were never out of the top three and any disappointment at being knocked out of the FA Cup in December by non-league Scunthorpe was forgotten five days later as they went to the top of the league. Back row (Left to right): G Mason, R Brook, W Morgan, V Brown, H Pearson, C McCaughey, H Boileau. Middle row: C Bisby, G McNestry, J Lauderdale, C Bourton, L Jones, A Fitton, H Webb. Front row: W Frith, W Lake, J Liddle.

ANXIETY—THEN TRIUMPH—AT HIGHFIELD ROAD

AFTER THE MATCH.—The crowd would not stop cheering until the players were brought from the dressing-rooms into the Directors' Box. Here they are shown listening to Alderman Fred Lee, President of the Club. Next to the President is Leslie Jones, whose fractured forearm has prevented him from playing since Easter Monday.

CITY PLAYERS "CHAIRED."—The scene at the end. Picture shows the crowd swarming on the field at the close of the game to "chair" the City players. Several minutes elapsed before the team could make its

MEMORABLE SCENES

Wild Scramble Follows City's Success

PLAYERS SWALLOWED UP IN "AVALANCHE"

WHO ever will forget the scenes at the close of Saturday's game at Highfield Road?

All the pent-up emotion of 90 minutes of anxiety, and finally triumph, was let loose in a roar of cheering which must have been heard miles away. Sensing what was likely to happen, the 22 players made a dive for the players' exit.

The Torquay men managed to escape without hindrance, and one or two City players as well, but the rest were swallowed up in the avalanche of people who seized their opportunity of displaying their joy in no uncertain manner. Curtis, Bourton, Elliott, Frith, McNestry, Liddle, and others were hauled into the air and carried by excited "fans." Hundreds of hands sought to pat them on the back, shake hands with them—anything to touch these idols.

For a while a mad scramble ensued, but then the crowd's good sense enabled their better judgment to overcome their ecstasy, and yard by yard the "chaired" players were carried to the entrance to the dressing room.

CONGRATULATORY SPEECHES

The players safely inside, the spectators on the field then turned their attention to the directors' box in the main stand, where Alderman Fred Lee, President of the club stood in front of a microphone, installed for the occasion by Messrs. Hanson. It was a long time before the cheering died down, and as preparation was made for the congratulatory speechmaking the crowd began to chant "We want Mason."

Their request was soon answered, for Alderman Lee announced that the Chairman, Mr. F. Bringer, had gone to fetch the players, a statement that was met by renewed cheers. These became more deafening than ever when a minute or two later the triumphant City team was led into the box by George Mason and Leslie Jones, both of whom were unable to play owing to injury. Trainer "Dick" Hill was also in the number.

"What a happy moment we live in," said Alderman Lee when at length the cheering subsided for a moment. "After years of toil," he continued, "we have just achieved the greatest success in the history of Coventry City F.C." (Cheers.)

"We congratulate Torquay for the splendid game they have given us. There was no 12 goals about (presumably referring to the Luton defeat of Bristol Rovers on Easter Monday). We have had to fight from start to finish. I am sure this afternoon you all feel so proud that in the first place you want to congratulate the players. They have worked so hard acting in unison, and have always fought like gentlemen for the success of Coventry City." (Cheers.)

MASON'S GREAT RECEPTION

George Mason had a great reception when he advanced to the microphone in response to the repeated demand. He was obviously too overcome by the occasion to say much. He managed to thank all concerned for their reception on behalf of the team. "I hope we do

May 1936. The Midland Daily Telegraph reports the finest day in the club's history at that point. There are memorable scenes as the Bantams clinch the Division 3 (South) championship with a nail-biting last day win over Torquay United. City missed a penalty then went a goal down before Ernie Curtis converted a second penalty and the goal king Bourton scored a late winner. The 30,000 crowd spilled onto the pitch and roared for their heroes. The title, though, had been won over Easter in two enthralling games with their closest rivals, Luton. A 1-1 draw at Kenilworth Road was followed two days later by a tense 0-0 draw at Highfield Road, watched by a record 42,975 crowd with hundreds locked out.

PLAYERS WHO HAVE PUT COVENTRY CITY ON TOP

Here are the Players who have been chiefly responsible for putting the City where they are to-day.

Back Row (left to right): Pearson, Astley, Morgan, Smith, Brown.
Second Row: Trainer Bruton, Jones, Boileau, Frith, Curtis, Mason, Fitton, Mr. Harry Storer (Secretary-Manager), Trainer Hill.
Front Row: McCaughey, McNestry, Lauderdale, Bourton, Lake, Liddle, Elliott.

The players who brought Division 2 football back to the city after a gap of eleven years. Back row (left to right): H Pearson, J Astley, W Morgan, B Smith, V Brown. Middle row: L Bruton (assistant trainer), L Jones, H Boileau, W Frith, E Curtis, G Mason, A Fitton, H Storer, R Hill (trainer). Front row: C McCaughey, Storer's dog, G McNestry, J Lauderdale, C Bourton, W Lake, J Liddle, C Elliott.

Clarrie Bourton never emulated the scoring feats of his first two seasons at the club but still managed to score 25 goals in 1933-34, 29 the following season and 25 in the promotion season. In Division 2, however, he found it harder to score and early in the 1937-38 season he was sold to Plymouth Argyle. In total he scored 172 league and 9 cup goals, a club record which will never be bettered.

The close season of 1936 and there is substantial work on the ground in preparation for the higher division. The 'rotting planks' of the old John Bull stand dating back to 1899 have been demolished and replaced with the Atkinson's Main stand costing £14,000. Concrete terracing is being laid on the Kop to replace the shale bank. The capacity of the ground was then 40,000 and in the halcyon seasons before the outbreak of war there would be several gates over that figure.

The players take a break from training to pose for a photograph with the club horse, Ginger. Prior to the purchase of a tractor in the late 1930s Ginger pulled the rollers and mowers over the pitch.

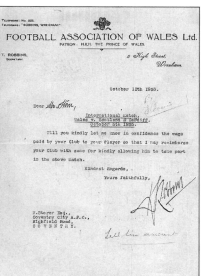

Leslie Jones was Bourton's striking partner between 1934 and 1937 and scored 74 goals in 144 games, even outscoring Clarrie in 1934-35 season. City resisted a £7,000 bid from Spurs in 1936 but in October 1937 he was sold to Arsenal in a controversial transfer, with City receiving £1,500 plus Bobby Davidson. City, unbeaten and top of Division 2, stuttered without him and missed out on promotion, whilst Jones helped Arsenal win the league championship.

Goalkeeper Alf Wood signed for City in 1935 and was understudy to Bill Morgan up until World War II, appearing for the first team only twice in four years. After the war he became the first choice keeper and appeared in 218 consecutive league games between 1946 and 1951. After a spell with Northampton he returned to Highfield Road as a trainer but in 1958 during an injury crisis he made twelve appearances as a 43 year old, the oldest City player in history.

First Public Trial

STRIPES v. WHITES

Saturday, August 15th, 1936
KICK-OFF 3-15 p.m.

TEAMS FOR TO-DAY'S MATCH

STRIPES

Right   Left

Morgan
1

Astley   Smith
2   3

Frith   Mason   Archer
4   5   6

Pritchard   Lauderdale   Lager   Lake   Fitton
7   8   9   10   11

Referee: Linesmen:
Mr. T. OWEN.   Mr. L. V. Wyles.
                Mr. F. Hudson.

Liddle   Jones   Bourton   MacDonald   McNestry
12   13   14   15   16

Curtis   Crawley   Snape
17   18   19

Boileau   Brown
20   21

Pearson
22

Left   Right

WHITES

The traditional pre-season public trial match took place on the Saturday before the start of the season. In the 1936 game the first-team defence (the Stripes) face the first-team attack (the Whites). The Stripes ran out 7-5 winners with the veteran Jock Lauderdale scoring a hat-trick in front of 6,500.

Harry Storer's interest in cricket rubbed off on his players and the club could put out a very useful side in the late 1930s. Here they are at Bedworth for a charity match in June 1937. (Left to right): W McDonald, E Lager, A Fitton, C Bourton, H Boileau, A Wood, M McPhee, H Barratt, W Metcalf, V Brown.

In the 1936-37 season Coventry City and Aston Villa met for the first time in their history and produced two thrilling games. City ground out a 0-0 draw at Villa Park in October in front of 63,686. Here Fitton goes close with Villa's keeper Biddlestone an open-mouthed admirer. In the return in February watched by 39,808 City were at the peak of their form and Jackie Brown's goal won the game for them.

City won a rare international honour in 1937 when 19-year-old Jack 'Snapper' Snape was selected for England v Scotland in a junior international, the equivalent of an Under-21 cap now. A month later he made his debut as feisty wing-half in a 2-1 win at Newcastle. He became a regular after the war and played over 100 games for City.

July 1937 and four of City's stars of the era share a joke. After letters to the Coventry Evening Telegraph criticising the team's scruffy appearance, a new kit was introduced with distinctive blue-white-blue panels and the players show it off at the photo session. From the left, new signing Walter Metcalf, a left-back from Brentford, goalkeeper Bill Morgan, a renowned practical joker, Clarrie Bourton, soon to be sold to Plymouth, and Billy McDonald.

July 1937. The complete professional playing staff in the new kit. Back row (left to right): C Elliott, L Jones, J Archer, A Wood, T Crawley, V Brown, C Bourton. Second row: R Hill (trainer), M McPhee, J Astley, E Lager, W Morgan, G Mason, D Tooze, W Metcalf, L Bruton. (assistant trainer). Third row: W Frith, G McNestry, J Brown, J Snape, H Storer, L Armeson, W Lake, B Smith, H Boileau. Sitting: E Roberts, W McDonald, Kyle, H Barratt, L Conwell, H Pearson, A Fitton.

August 1937 and the pre-season public trial match. Coventry-born youngster Harry Barratt, playing for the Reds, shoots for goal past George Mason playing for the Stripes. The game ended 3-3 with new signing Magnus McPhee from Bradford Park Avenue hitting a hat-trick for the Stripes. McPhee only played 12 games for the club, scoring six goals but during and after the war he was a prolific scorer for Reading.

Billy McDonald joined the club from Tranmere in the summer of 1936 as a scheming inside-forward, having previously played for Manchester United. He had two good seasons but a loss of form in 1938-39 persuaded Harry Storer to sell him to Plymouth in the summer of 1939. Sadly the outbreak of war meant he never appeared for Argyle.

1937-38 season saw the departure of 'the goal machine' Clarrie Bourton and years later the Birmingham Sports Argus commemorated his career in their Where are they now series.

The club programme displays a prominent bantam on its cover with the brewers Mitchell and Butlers also featuring heavily. This programme was issued for the home game against Sheffield Wednesday in November 1937 when City, unbeaten in 15 games since the start of the season, lost their record to the visitors. City were never out of the top four but missed out on promotion by one point.

30 October 1937. A 'light meal' before a 'heavy task'. The City team prepare for their top of the table clash at Villa Park with a pre-match meal at the Kings Head. From left to right: E Lager, E Roberts, W Morgan, H Barratt, W Frith (partially hidden), W Metcalf, trainer R Hill (standing), J Astley, G Mason (hidden), J Archer, W McDonald, J Brown. A crowd of 67,271, at the time a record gate for a Division 2 game, watched a 1-1 draw.

Bobby Davidson (second from right) has a final try-out before the FA Cup-tie with York City in January 1938. Davidson passed a fitness test but City lost at Third Division York. Also pictured are (left to right) Vic Brown, Charlie Elliott, and Laurie Conwell, who had deputised for the injured Davidson. Davidson joined City as part of the deal that took Les Jones to Arsenal but the Scottish inside forward never displayed the form of his earlier career.

Following page: After training, the team retired to the players' lounge to play cards or darts. A youthful Harry Barratt (sixth from left) watches the dapper Walter Metcalf, in his plus fours, throw the dart. A hirsute Alf Wood (second from right) keeps his cards close to his chest whilst the pipe-smoking Les Warner admires his hand.

Chapter 4.

Coventry City's ambitions for a place in Division One went on hold in September 1939 for seven years. World War II meant there was no competitive football. Friendlies were played at Highfield Road until the ground was severely bombed, like most of the city, in November 1940. Although the ground was patched up and able to stage friendlies again in 1942 the sport effectively came to a standstill.

As hostilities came to halt in 1945 Harry Storer was tempted away to manage Birmingham City and was succeeded by his trusted assistant Dick Bayliss. Sadly, Bayliss became the only City manager to die in service in 1947 when, during the worst winter in living memory, he caught a chill during a nightmare drive home from a scouting trip and died some weeks later. Former player Billy Frith took over and steered the club to eighth place, thanks to 29 goals from George Lowrie, but he failed to improve the team's position the following season. Frith was sacked in November 1948 after City had lost ten of their first sixteen matches and Harry Storer returned from Birmingham, inspiring five straight wins. Relegation was avoided but the following season the magic of Storer failed to work and it needed several new signings and an eight-match unbeaten end to the season to avoid relegation.

The 1950-51 season was a throwback to the 1930s, with exciting attacking football and a settled side. By Christmas, City were top of the table and looked set for promotion until disaster struck. Storer paid a club record £20,000 for the free-scoring Tommy Briggs from Grimsby to replace the local hero Ted Roberts. In what can only be described as 'player power', the team slumped, winning only one of six games and thoughts of promotion disappeared fast. Briggs was dropped but the damage was done. City finished seventh and their best post-war chance of making the top flight was gone.

Nine seasons of Second Division football came to an end in 1951-52 when an ageing side failed to reproduce the previous season's form. Storer gambled by re-signing Lowrie and then later striker Eddie Brown and defender Roy Kirk but it was a case of too little, too late and City were relegated at Leeds on the final day of the season. Nemo wrote in the Coventry Evening Telegraph: 'unless there is a bold, progressive policy from now on City will have a Third Division side for a number of years.' It was prophetic - the club did not have a bold policy and they would not return to Division Two for twelve years.

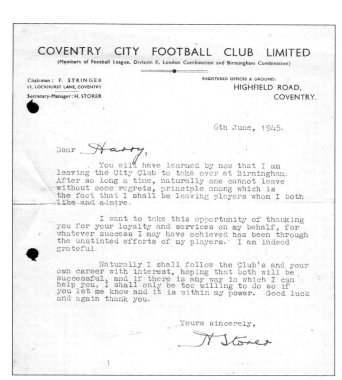

COVENTRY CITY FOOTBALL CLUB LIMITED
(Members of Football League, Division II, London Combination and Birmingham Combination)

Chairman: F. STRINGER
13, LOCKHURST LANE, COVENTRY

REGISTERED OFFICES & GROUND:
HIGHFIELD ROAD,
COVENTRY.

Secretary-Manager: H. STORER

6th June, 1945.

Dear Harry,

You will have learned by now that I am leaving the City Club to take over at Birmingham. After so long a time, naturally one cannot leave without some regrets, principle among which is the fact that I shall be leaving players whom I both like and admire.

I want to take this opportunity of thanking you for your loyalty and services on my behalf, for whatever success I may have achieved has been through the unstinted efforts of my players. I am indeed grateful.

Naturally I shall follow the Club's and your own career with interest, hoping that both will be successful, and if there is any way in which I can help you, I shall only be too willing to do so if you let me know and it is within my power. Good luck and again thank you.

Yours sincerely,

H Storer

Weeks after the end of World War II Harry Storer was lured away to be Birmingham's new manager. At the time it was a major surprise but he had certainly done his homework and inherited a much younger and stronger squad of players than he had left at Highfield Road. In his first season Birmingham won the Football League (South) and reached the FA Cup semi-finals, and two years later won promotion to Division 1. Storer's touching letter to Harry Barratt belies the public image of the man as a tyrannical leader feared by his players.

A rare picture of a wartime game at Highfield Road. West Brom are the visitors and Barratt is pressing the keeper in case of an error.

Dick Bayliss, Storer's chief scout and right-hand man since 1931, took over as manager in June 1945. Here he gives a pep talk to his team during the transitional 1945-46 season.

In May 1946 City travelled to Denmark for a series of friendly matches against local clubs. The team pose before their opening game against Aarhus, in which goals from Harry Barratt and Alf Setchell gave them a 2-1 victory. The players shown are back row (left to right): D Tooze, A Wood, W Metcalf. Middle row: G Mason, J Snape, T Crawley. Front row: D Simpson, H Barratt, E Roberts, E Aldecoa, A Setchell. Dick Bayliss is leaning on Crawley's shoulder.

ARSENAL FOOTBALL CLUB, LTD.
OFFICIAL PROGRAMME.

SEPTEMBER, 1945

Price:—ONE PENNY.

FOOTBALL LEAGUE (South)	FOOTBALL LEAGUE (South)
On Saturday, September 8th	On Wednesday, September 12th
ARSENAL v. LUTON	**SPURS v. LEICESTER CITY**
Kick-off 3 p.m.	Kick-off 6 p.m.

FOOTBALL LEAGUE (South)   Sat., 1st Sept., 1945.   **Kick-off 3 p.m.**

ARSENAL

Red Shirts, White Sleeves and Collars ; Knickers White; Stockings Blue, White Rings and White Tops.

RIGHT WING.   LEFT WING.

1
W. Griffiths
Goal

2   3
Scott   Barnes
Right Back   Left Back

4   5   6
Horsfield   Smith, L.   Wade
Right Half   Centre Half   Left Half

7   8   9   10   11
Farquhar   Nelson   Mortensen   Holland   Wrigglesworth
Outside Right Inside Right Centre   Inside Left   Outside Left

Referee—Mr. C. J. BARRICK
Linesmen   Mr. L. G. AYLOTT (Blue and White Flag)
Mr. S. J. ISOM (Red and White Flag).

11   10   9   8   7
Gardner   Lewis   Lowrie   Barratt   Pritchard
Outside Left   Inside Left   Centre   Inside Right   Outside Right

6   5   4
Crawley   Mason (Capt.)   Snape
Left Half   Centre Half   Right Half

3   2
Metcalfe   Elliott
Left Back   Right Back

1
Wood
Goal

LEFT WING   RIGHT WING.

COVENTRY CITY
Blue Shirts.   White Knickers.

ANY ALTERATION WILL BE NOTED ON THE BOARD.

After the war there was one transitional season run on a regional basis which saw City in the Football League (South) playing with First and Second division teams from London and the Midlands. It meant City's first ever meeting with the famous Arsenal. On the opening day of the season City beat the Gunners 2-0 at Highfield Road and a week later achieved an excellent draw in London. Whilst the single-sheet programme doesn't mention the fact, the game was actually played at White Hart Lane, as Highbury was used as an ARP centre. Arsenal were without many of their stars who were still on service duty but had a useful guest centre-forward called Stan Mortensen from Blackpool.

Trainer Dick Hill puts the team through its paces on a rather ragged looking Highfield Road pitch.

COVENTRY CITY. F.C. 1946-7

DOBBS   COX   TOOZE   Mr HITCHENER (SECRETARY)   WOOD   MASON   WYKES   CRAWLEY
TRAINER.F.HILL   WARNER   ROBERTS   Mr BAYLISS (MANAGER)   SMITH.N   SETCHELL   ASST.TRAINER MORGAI
BETT   ALDECOA   BARRATT   YOUNG   SMITH.S.

League football resumed in August 1946 and City have two new faces - Spanish refugee Emilio Aldecoa, a goalscoring winger, and Fred Bett, an inside-forward signed from Sunderland. Apart from them, the squad comprised pre-war players and a handful of local players who had kept the club going through the war.

The austere times of 1946 saw many everyday items in short supply and severely rationed. Paper was no exception but the club managed to put out an eight-page programme on flimsy paper. This is the first home game of the season against West Brom, won 3-2 with two goals from Barratt and one from Bett. The programme apologises to the fans for the large holes in the roof of the covered end but explains that until the Government gives the all-clear the work to carry out repairs cannot commence.

A training session on Warwick racecourse in the autumn of 1946 in fetching polo-neck sweaters.

City's first post-war star, George Lowrie, the heir to Clarrie Bourton's crown. He scored on his debut on the last Saturday of peacetime soccer in 1939, in a game made void, and had to wait seven years for his full debut. He peaked in 1946-47, scoring 29 goals in 36 games, including four hat-tricks and was sold to Newcastle for a record £18,500 in March 1948.

January 1947. City players have fun on Blackpool beach with a lifebelt in preparation for their FA Cup 4th round tie at Burnley.

February 1948 and Newcastle are the visitors. Harry Barratt can't stop the winger getting his cross over and Jack Snape looks on. City, however, are good value for a point against the league leaders. Lowrie scored his last goal before his big move to the North East.

Back Row: Tooze, D., Mason, G., Snape, J., Wood, A., Hill, R. (Trainer), Dearson, D., Barratt, H., Mason. R.
Sitting: Warner, L., Simpson, D. E., Roberts, E., Mr. W. Frith (Manager),
Davidson, R. T., Setchell, A., Ashall, C.
On Ground: Lowrie, G.

A happy looking squad with new manager Billy Frith. The only newcomer is Welsh international Don Dearson, signed from Birmingham the previous March. George Ashall (first from the right, sitting) broke his leg in an early season home game against West Brom and never played again.

The Red House team coach awaits as the Bantams prepare for a trip to Hillsborough in February 1949. Left to right: Unknown, H Storer, R Hill (trainer), N Lockhart, W Morgan (assistant trainer), I Jamieson, H Barratt, D Simpson, unknown, L Warner, G Mason (partially hidden), D Dearson, J Snape, A Wood, R Mason, unknown, P Hill. Peter Hill is set to make his debut as a 17-year-old and went on to make 303 appearances for the club over 13 years. He later became first-team trainer.

August 1948. A new striped kit replaces the panelled shirts but stormclouds were hovering and in the November after only one win in twelve games Frith is sacked and Harry Storer returns as manager.

April 1949. Reserve centre-forward Jack Evans is called up for his debut against Fulham and scores the only goal of the game. The form of Ted Roberts restricted Evans to eight appearances in four years and he was released in 1952 never having repeated his goalscoring feat.

September 1949. City pictured before a 1-1 draw at Preston. Peter Murphy has become the new star and would be sold to Spurs at the end of the season. Ian Jamieson was Storer's first signing after his return and would later become a director. Back row (left to right): L Cook, C Timmins, G Mason, A Wood, R Mason, N Simpson, R Hill (trainer). Front row: L Warner, I Jamieson, P Murphy, P Hill, N Lockhart.

A cartoon from the era which perfectly captures the mood of Coventry fans of the late 1940s. The unfulfilled dreams of the pre-war years were fading as each year went by and 1949-50 was another season of frustration as the club became embroiled in a serious relegation battle.

February 1950 and City face four tough games in the relegation scrap. The first target is achieved - an amazing 3-0 home win over promotion candidates Sheffield Wednesday. Away draws were achieved at Southampton and Bury before the leaders Spurs ended the mini-run. It needed five straight wins in April to pull City out of their freefall and avoid the drop.

Caricatures of two of the most popular players of the era. Lockhart was an Irish international left-winger who joined City in 1947 and played 189 games in five years. Wood missed his first game since the war in April 1951 at the age of 36. Early the following season he was released, judged to be 'over the hill'.

ALF WOOD (Coventry)

NORMAN LOCKHART. (COVENTRY CITY)

August 1950. City's captain Harry Barratt shakes hands with Notts County's Deans on the opening day of the season. Over 41,000 watch City beat newly promoted County, who had Tommy Lawton in their ranks, 2-0 with goals from Les 'Plum' Warner and Ken Chisholm.

Chisholm goes close with a diving header against Notts County.

September 1950. City travel to Gigg Lane to play Bury. Martin McDonnell has taken over at centre-half from George Mason. A settled start has made an excellent start to the season but City lose 0-1 to the Shakers. Back row (left to right): C Timmins, H Barratt, M McDonnell, A Wood, N Simpson, R Mason. Front row: L Warner, I Jamieson, E Roberts, K Chisholm, N Lockhart.

October 1950. City are riding high and almost 35,000 see them beat league leaders Blackburn 6-1. Lockhart scores after 20 seconds and the result is never in doubt. City second in the table.

City travel to Sunderland for an FA Cup third round tie as leaders of Division 2 and despite a brave fight and an heroic goalkeeping display by Alf Wood lose 0-2 to an impressive home team. Their league form suffers and one win in six games sees their promotion hopes fade.

A telegram wishing the team luck in their FA Cup-tie at Roker Park.

On a snowbound pitch Notts County gain revenge for their opening day defeat, becoming the first side to lower City's colours at home in the 1950-51 season. Two goals in the first fifteen minutes from Tommy Lawton are enough and the visitors win 2-1. McDonnell and Chisholm struggle to contain the awesome Lawton.

Captain Harry Barratt and Alf Wood lead the team out at Upton Park. At 32-years of age Harry's injuries are more frequent and in less than a year his first class career will be over. Wood, three years older, will continue playing for eight years.

Messrs Barratt, Mason and Wood receive benefit cheques from the club chairman Jones in recognition of their service to the club. Timmins, Dick Mason, Lockhart and McDonnell look on enviously.

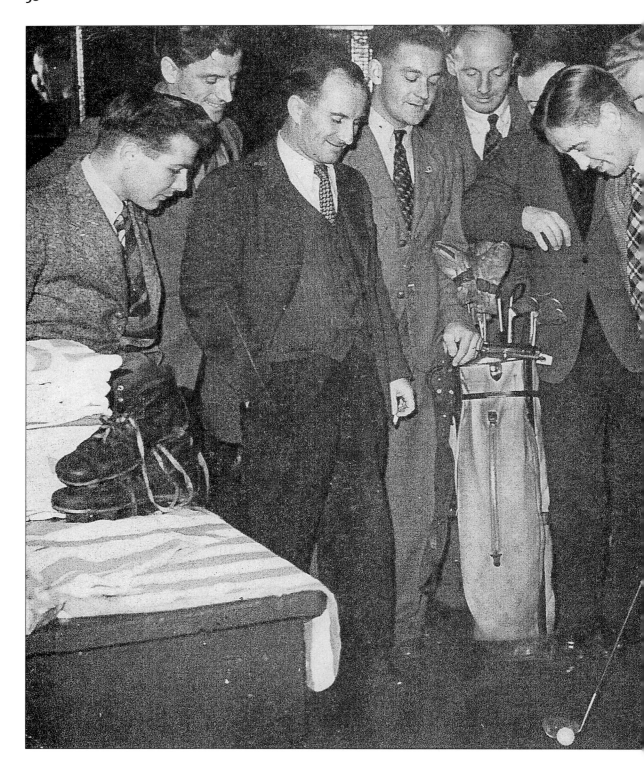

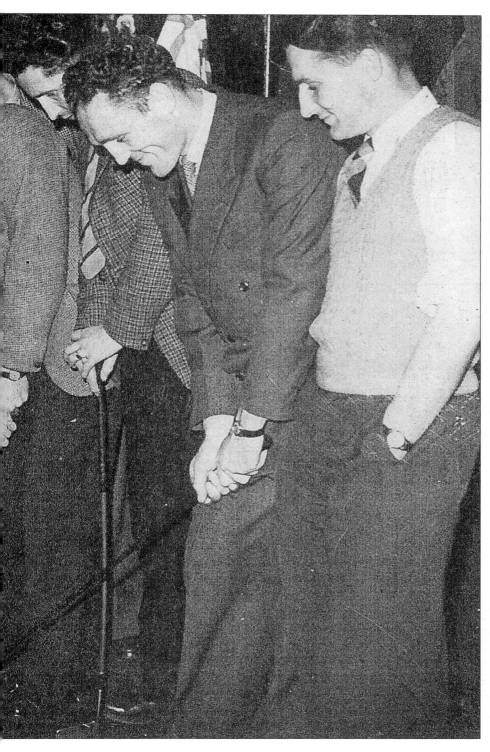

Fun in the dressing room. Les Cook (left) and Martin McDonnell demonstrate their golf stances watched by an admiring bunch of players. Cook was a useful utility player between 1949 and 1955 making 94 appearances before injury wrecked his career. He later appeared for Rugby Town. McDonnell made 232 appearances between 1949 and 1955 initially as a right-back then later as the regular centre-half. He joined Harry Storer at Derby in 1955 and was later an estate agent in Coventry.

Coventry Evening Telegraph, Saturday, March 15, 1952 3

The 1951-52 season proved to be a disastrous one for the club. Rarely out of the bottom three all season, Father Time had caught up with so many of the players. Ironically a year earlier they had looked good promotion candidates. Three wins out of four in February appeared to have turned things round but a 3-1 home defeat to Leicester, with Arthur Rowley scoring twice prompted the Coventry Evening Telegraph to publish a cartoon illustrating the club's plight. The Third Division abyss was yawning and the reasons for their plight were numerous.

Coventry Evening Telegraph, Saturday, March 22, 1952 3

On transfer deadline day in a last desperate attempt to avoid relegation manager Storer signed Roy Kirk, a centre-half from Leeds, and Eddie Brown, a centre-forward from Southampton. Storer is depicted as a wartime ARP man trying to cool the volcano down and relying on his new recruits. Brown scored on his home debut as Brentford were beaten 1-2 but only two wins in the last seven games condemned City to relegation.

Chapter 5.

If Coventry City fans thought that life in Division Three would be a bed of roses following relegation they had a major shock. For the next six years there was little to celebrate at Highfield Road. The Bantams were never in contention for promotion and the club staggered from one disaster to another and got through seven managers in six years. Storer remained in charge during the 1952-53 season and despite fifteen home wins average gates slumped from 22,000 to 13,000. Norman Lockhart became the first of many outstanding players to be sold during the era as financial survival became the priority.

In November 1953 Storer left the club: the official line was that he had resigned but many knew that he had been sacked. Jack Fairbrother arrived as the new manager in January 1954 but within two months suffered personal tragedy when his wife died in a fall at home. Before the season was over an attendance of 4,785 was recorded, the lowest for 30 years, and revolution was in the air. After a noisy AGM the board under H G Jones resigned and Erle Shanks, a driving force in the 1930s returned as chairman.

Fairbrother lasted until October 1954 when just weeks after top scorer Eddie Brown was sold, he resigned for 'health reasons'. Shanks had paid off a large amount of the club's debt and he was calling the shots.

Former player Charlie Elliott acted as caretaker until Jesse Carver arrived in the summer of 1955. Shanks lured Carver away from Roma and made him the highest paid manager in the Football League. He arrived in a blaze of publicity but despite some stylish home displays the classy football was not designed for the rigours of Division Three. Carver resigned and returned to Italy, leaving George Raynor, his number two and former Swedish coach, in charge.

Raynor was only manager until June, when Harry Warren arrived and Raynor was demoted to coach. November proved the turning point: first Raynor resigned, then Reg Matthews was sold to Chelsea for £22,000. The season was the worst in 30 years, with a final position of sixteenth.

The 1957-58 season was of vital importance as the regionalised Third Division was being reorganised and only the top twelve sides in the Northern and Southern sections would form the new Division Three. After a poor start Warren was sacked and Billy Frith returned but failed to arrest a slump which ended with City in nineteenth place and founder members of the basement division. The boardroom wranglings continued with Walter Brandish taking over as chairman from a disillusioned Shanks.

The ignominy of playing clubs like Hartlepool, Darlington and York City hit home hard and Frith, managing on a shoestring budget got promotion at the first attempt. Shrewd buys like Reg Ryan, George Stewart, Arthur Lightening and Ray Straw thrilled the crowds which returned in great numbers, with five gates over 20,000.

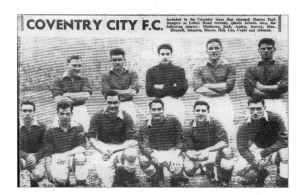

In two seasons of Division 3 football many of the old faces had disappeared from the scene to be replaced by a youthful team. Reg Matthews, Frank Austin, Lol Harvey and Peter Hill all came through the club's junior ranks. Another City product, Gordon Nutt, was sold to Cardiff for £15,000 and £10,000 of the fee was spent on 34-year-old former England centre-forward Jack Lee from Derby. It was bad business. Lee played only 15 games before retiring through injury. When this picture was taken at QPR in January 1955, Charlie Elliott was caretaker-manager following the departure of Jack Fairbrother the previous October. A week earlier however, the club had announced that Jesse Carver, the manager of AS Roma, would be joining City as manager in the summer. Back row (left to right): L Harvey, F Austin, R Matthews, M McDonnell, R Kirk. Front row: A Moore, P Hill, J Lee, N Simpson, E Johnson, T Capel. City are in their change red shirts.

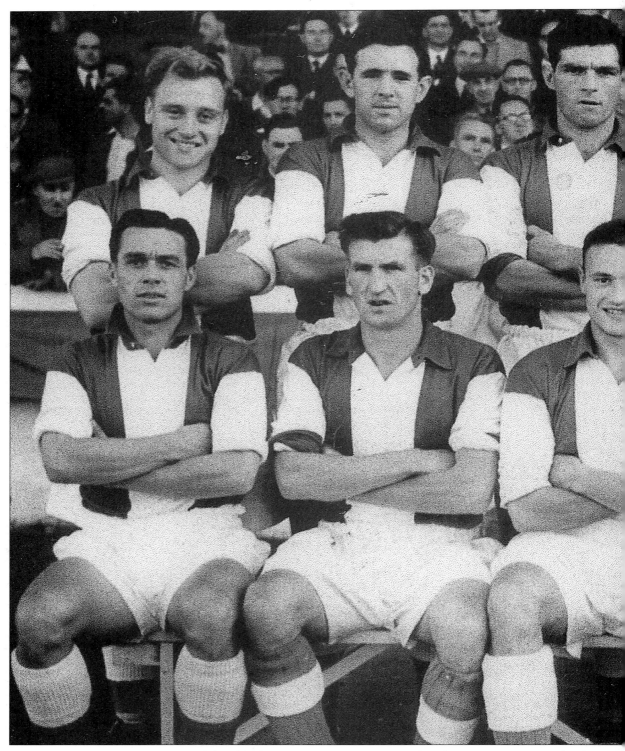

September 1955. Carver is in the manager's chair and the football is a joy to behold. City are unbeatable at home but their away form is dire. Carver also gives youth its head with six home grown players in this line-up against Gillingham, a game City won 2-0 with goals from youngsters Charlie Dutton and Ray Sambrook. Back row (left to right): L Harvey, K Jones, R Kirk, R Matthews, N Simpson, F Austin. Front row: A Moore, B Hawkings, C Dutton, R Sambrook, J Hill.

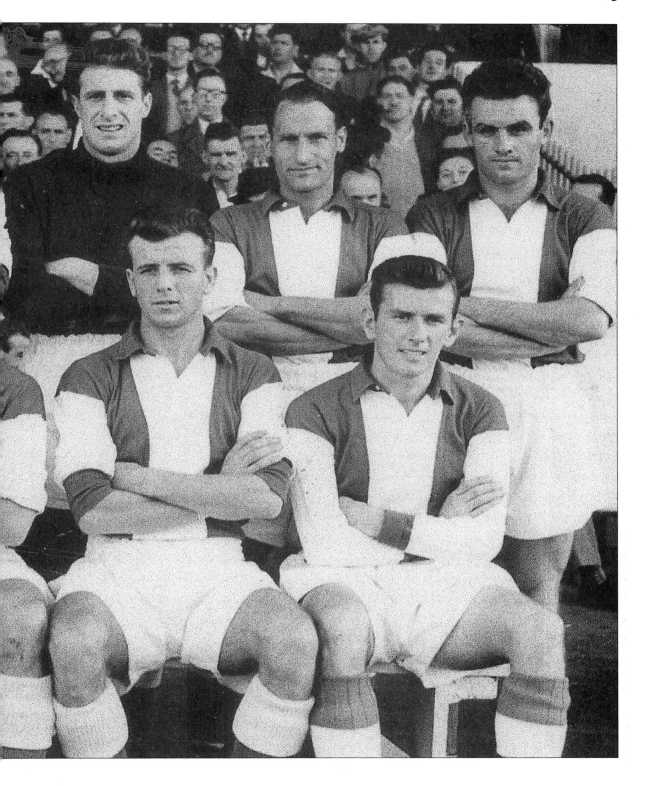

January 1956. Leyton Orient are the visitors in the first home game since Carver controversially left to return to Italy. Carver's only two signings, Ken McPherson and Dennis Uphill, are shown here as City attack and both scored in the 3-0 win. City's first floodlights, officially opened in 1953 with a game against Scottish club Queen of the South, are in evidence on the roof of the stand.

City's most famous player of the 1950s was local-born goalkeeper Reg Matthews who won five England caps as a Division 3 player in 1956. His consistent form over two seasons brightened the gloom at Highfield Road. Here at Walsall in April 1956, a week before his England debut at Hampden Park, he has this shot safely covered.

Reg Matthews' England badge. In his five internationals he never appeared on the losing side as England beat Brazil 4-2, Germany 3-1 in Berlin and drew with Scotland, Sweden and Northern Ireland.

Matthews' fifth and last international was against Northern Ireland in Belfast in October 1956. For no apparent reason he was not selected for the next international and Reg, fearing that his international career would be hindered as a Division 3 player, asked for a transfer. A month after the Irish game he was sold to Chelsea for £22,000, a world record fee for a goalkeeper. Ironically Reg was never picked for England again. England team in Belfast, back row (left to right): Ronnie Clayton, Jeff Hall, Don Revie, Reg Matthews, Roger Byrne, Duncan Edwards. Front row: Stanley Matthews, Tommy Taylor, Billy Wright, Denis Wilshaw, Colin Grainger.

THE ENGLAND TEAM v. IRELAND
Back row: R. Clayton, J. Hall, D. Revie, R. D. Matthews, R. Byrne, D. Edwards
Front row: S. Matthews, T. Taylor, W. A. Wright, D. Wilshaw, C. Grainger

REG. MATTHEWS

REG MATTHEWS Coventry City

Matthews' fame in the era was recognised by the cigarette and bubble gum companies who issued cards with his caricature and his photograph in the yellow England jersey.

April 1956. Matthews is on international duty and, with reserve keeper Alf Bentley injured, 40-year-old assistant trainer Alf Wood is recalled after a five-year absence for the final game of the season against Reading. He has little to do in a 0-0 draw and here comfortably catches a cross watched by City players (left to right in stripes): Noel Simpson, Jim Regan and Frank Austin.

The Dell was a graveyard for the Bantams in the 1950s with only two points gained in nine visits. In February 1958 with City looking set to finish in the bottom of half of Division 3 (South) and thus be 'relegated' to the new Division 4, they suffered their worst defeat, 1-7. City's heroic young goalkeeper Graham Spratt saved City from an ever bigger defeat but his nerves were so shattered that he only played two more games for the club. Roy Kirk looks on as Derek Reeves heads home.

In the washing room at Highfield Road
the two ladies, both called Mrs
Bradshaw, put the players kit through
the mangle and provide a good advert
for Surf.

A scene from the Players' Recreation room in the 1950s.

**March 1958. Ray Hill's brief moment of glory. The Stourbridge-born forward scores the first of his two goals in a 2-2 draw with Brighton.
City's number 9, Ray Straw, is desperately trying to get out of the way whilst 20-year old-debutant goalkeeper, Dave Hollins, brother of
John, closes his eyes. Hill played only 14 games for the Bantams, scoring five goals, but soon after, along with Peter Hill and Brian Hill,
created a unique record at Gillingham when three players with the same surname appeared for the club.**

The City team pose on the eve of the 1958-59 season in which they will be inaugural members of the new Division 4. Billy Frith had returned to the club the previous September but they had been unable to avoid finishing below halfway in Division 3 (South). Back Row (left to right): B Shepherd, R Kirk, G Spratt, J Sanders, T Brindley, G Curtis, A Wood (trainer), J Knox, R Straw. Middle row: W Frith (manager), B Nicholas, J Rogers, V Griffiths, P Hill, R Hill, W Copping (coach). Front row: F Austin, D Smith, B Hill, M Walters, M Kearns, L Harvey, E Jones.

August 1958. City struggle to a 0-0 draw with Darlington on the opening day of the season. Vernon Griffiths heads for goal watched by Ray Straw and Frank Austin. Over 15,000, the highest gate in the Division watched the game. After three games City are 91st in the league.

September 1958. Jimmy Rogers challenges the Exeter keeper. Rogers had an amazing autumn scoring 13 goals in 17 games, including seven goals in two games against Aldershot within ten days. He had also scored another hat-trick against the Shots the previous season. In December he was transferred back to Bristol City, the club he had left to join Coventry in December 1956.

Reg Ryan, affectionately known as Paddy, runs out for his City debut against Exeter. The 32-year-old Eire international was an inspired purchase by manager Frith who immediately made him captain. The team lost only three of the next 21 games and his midfield probing and experience were a major factor in the promotion success that season.

November 1958. Weight-training under the Main Stand. Lol Harvey, Peter Hill, Roy Kirk, Brian Nicholas and George Curtis are led through their routines by an unknown trainer.

Promoted to Division 3 by virtue of finishing runners-up in Division 4, City pose for a celebration photo with the proud board of directors. Back row (left to right): K Cornbill, M Walters, V Griffiths, R Sheppard, G Stewart, R Farmer, R Ryan, A Daley, P Wyer, L Harvey. Second row: A Wood (trainer), R Kirk, K Satchwell, R Hill, R Straw, R Wesson, A Lightening, G Spratt, unknown, F Kletz, M Kearns, G Curtis, W Copping (coach). Third row: B Hitchiner (secretary), P Mead (director), F Stringer (director), D Robins (vice-chairman), Dr P Coghill (medical officer), W Frith (manager). Front row: B Shepherd, B Nicholas, B Hill, P Hill, J Boxley, F Austin.

Chapter 6.

After winning promotion from Division Four at the first attempt City looked like going straight through to Division Two, losing only one of their first eleven games and lying in third place at Easter. Three successive defeats over the holiday period put paid to the promotion hopes and the fans repeated the 1938 gripe that money should have been made available to strengthen the team.

The following season was a grave disappointment with only a brave Cup defeat at Anfield to cheer the fans. By this time Derrick Robins had become chairman and made money available for players but Billy Frith was unable to use it wisely. In November 1961 City were struggling and, four days after an embarrassing FA Cup defeat at home to Kings Lynn, Frith was out and Jimmy Hill arrived.

That season petered out with little seemingly changed, but behind the scenes the Sky Blue revolution was under way with the first step being the introduction of an all-Sky Blue continental kit. In the close season Robins' £30,000 gift for new players was wisely spent by Hill and, with Terry Bly scoring regularly, the promotion push began to take shape, only to be interrupted by some of the worst winter weather of the century. An epic Cup run was ended by Manchester United and when league action was resumed the fixture backlog took its toll and City finished fourth.

Season ticket sales boomed and expectation was high in the summer of 1963 and the Sky Blues swept all before them in a feast of attacking football with gates averaging almost 26,000. However a nine-point lead at Christmas was frittered away and it took a final day victory over Colchester to clinch promotion and the Division Three championship.

In Division Two expectations were even higher and an amazing five-win start saw crowds nudging 40,000 and talk of promotion on everyone's lips. Although the team's form faded and it became a season of consolidation, off the field Hill and Robins transformed the club into one of the most modern in the country with a constant stream of ideas to promote the image of the club and foster the relationship with the fans. The Sky Blue express train helped carry some of the large away followings that were the envy of the big clubs. Pre-match entertainment was introduced with everything from sky divers to pop groups and Hill turned the Eton Boating Song into the Sky Blue Song.

Promotion was just missed in 1965-66 but the nucleus of the side was in place for a major assault on promotion. The final piece in the jigsaw was the £55,000 record signing of Ian Gibson, a natural successor to George Hudson, controversially sold, as the fans' favourite. After a shaky start the Sky Blues embarked on a 25-match unbeaten run which culminated in the Division Two championship, highlighted by the famous victory over Wolves in front of a record 51,455 Highfield Road crowd.

The Coventry Evening Telegraph

FOOTBALL

No. 21,918 [71st Year]   SATURDAY, NOVEMBER 25, 1961   THREEPENCE

Bottom of Southern League, But Linnets Chirp Merrily

WHAT A SHOCK – CITY OUT

RESULTS AT A GLANCE

F.A. CUP — Second Round

H.T.			
0-1	Aldershot 2	Brentford 2
0-1	Ashford 0	Q.P. Rangers . 3
1-0	Barnsley 1	Carlisle 2
0-2	Bridgwater 0	Crystal Palace 3
4-0	Bristol City .. 8	Dartford 2
0-1	Chester 0	Morecambe ... 1
1-1	Chesterfield ... 2	Oldham 2
1-2	Coventry City . 1	Kings Lynn ... 2
1-1	Crewe Alex. ... 1	Port Vale 1
0-1	Gateshead .:. 0	Workington .. 2

H.T.			
0-1	Hartlepools ... 2	Accrington ... 1
0-1	Hull City 0	Bradford City 2
1-0	Margate 1	Notts County 1
3-0	Northampton .. 3	Kettering 0
0-1	Rochdale 1	Wrexham 2
0-0	Romford 1	Watford 3
0-0	Shrewsbury ... 3	Brierley Hill .. 0
3-1	Southport 4	Mansfield T. .. 2
0-1	Torquay 1	Peterborough . 4
0-0	Weymouth 1	Newport 0

League—Division I

H.T.			
2-0	Aston Villa 2	Manchester C. 1
0-0	Blackburn 0	Fulham 2
1-1	Blackpool 1	Sheffield Wed. 3
0-2	Cardiff City ... 0	Ipswich T. ... 3
1-0	Chelsea 4	West Brom. ... 1

League—Division II

H.T.			
0-0	Brighton 0	Preston N.E. 0
0-0	Bristol Rovers 0	Middlesbro' ... 2
1-0	Bury 1	Plymouth 1
0-1	Charlton 0	Huddersfield .. 2
1-1	Leeds United .. 4	Walsall 1

Gift Goal Fails to Rouse Frith's Men

COVENTRY CITY 1, KING'S LYNN 2

KING'S LYNN, bottom club in the Premier Section of the Southern League, came up with one of the day's F.A. Cup second round shocks at Highfield Road this afternoon when they knocked out Coventry City. They gave a display of dash and skill which stunned City fans in the 12,080 crowd. Make no mistake about it — the gallant Linnets fully deserved their success against a City who were unbelievably poor and who were outfought and out-tackled by the part-timers.

It was the first time in 26 years that a non-League side have put City out of the Cup and, quite frankly, there was hardly any time this afternoon when City seemed likely to get on top of the Norfolk side. Even City's goal — the result of a mix-up between Lynn centre-half Hindle and his goalkeeper Manning —was a gift, but the Linnets shrugged it off with two goals within three minutes through Johnson and Wright to win a place in the third round.

King's Lynn amazed the crowd by keeping up their furious pace in the second-half and but for a stout defensive display by George Curtis things could have been much worse for City. This was the Linnets' finest hour and at the end there was a rush of fans to acclaim them as they jumped, arms out-

CUP REPORT
By Nemo

up an attack had a shot charged down and Imlach tore 60 yards high on the roof of the covered stand.

Peter Hill was twice too slow to get his line moving and was dispossessed and the second time it nearly landed his side in trouble for the left-back, Wilson, took the ball downfield and was only robbed near the by-line by Bennett.

After a disappointing 1960-61 season manager Frith was under pressure and a shock FA Cup defeat at the hands of Kings Lynn sealed his fate. The Linnets, bottom of the Southern League, outfought and out-tackled their league opponents and deservedly won.

The Coventry Evening Telegraph

LAST EDITION

No. 21,921 [71st Year]   WEDNESDAY, NOVEMBER 29, 1961   · · ·   2½d.

Clean Sweep at City Ground

Players' Leader is New Manager

Has Been Given 'Full Control'

JIMMY HILL TAKES OVER AT HIGHFIELD ROAD

Billy Frith, Trainers and Scout Dismissed

MR. JIMMY HILL, whose appointment as manager of Coventry City Football Club in place of Mr. Billy Frith was announced today, was at the Highfield Road ground this afternoon to meet the players.

He arrived with the club chairman, Mr. Derrick Robins, and within 45 minutes he was out on the ground in a track suit having a kick-about with some of the players, writes NEMO.

The statement earlier today, in which the directors of the club announced the dismissal of Mr. Frith,

Mr. Jimmy Hill and Mr. Derrick Robins at the City Football Ground

U.S. Puts Chimp into Orbit

A CHIMPANZEE was launched into orbit at Cape Canaveral today to pioneer America's first orbital flight by a man.

The capsule went into an orbit ranging from 86 to 127 nautical miles from the earth. (A nautical mile is 6,800ft.).

The capsule separated from the Atlas rocket and was soaring at an angle of 34 degrees, exactly as planned.

The space craft is planned to take the chimpanzee, called Enos,

Four days after the Kings Lynn debacle, Jimmy Hill is installed as the new manager. He had watched the game from the stands and would have been appointed even if they had won. Sacked with Frith are trainers Alf Wood and Ted Roberts and chief scout Arthur Jepson.

March 1963. Jimmy Hill's first full season in charge saw the newly nicknamed Sky Blues enjoy their best FA Cup run since 1910. They beat Lincoln, Portsmouth (after three games) and Sunderland, in an epic game at Highfield Road, to earn a quarter-final place against Manchester United. On a muddy pitch the skill of United won through, but not before City had taken the lead through Terry Bly. United won 3-1 and went on to win the trophy. Here Harry Gregg blocks Humphries' shot.

The 1963-64 promotion challenge ground to a halt in early 1964 with the Sky Blues - nine points clear at the New Year - failing to win any of 11 games between 3 January and 28 March. The fans, including the club's programme cartoon character, Sid Sky Blue, were getting jittery and in the two weeks prior to this cartoon Southend had won 5-2 at Highfield Road and Bournemouth had also beaten City, 2-1.

Syd Sky Blue says : "Listen, Woman ! Just because I keep jibbering in my sleep about Southend and Bournemouth, it doesn't mean we're going to the seaside for Easter."

George Hudson scores the vital goal against Colchester which secures the Third Division Championship in April 1964.

Brian Hill became the youngest ever City player in April 1958 when he made his debut against Gillingham aged 16 years 273 days, a record that stood for 41 years. He also scored on his debut, something he only repeated seven times in 282 appearances for the club. He played in all four divisions before moving to Torquay in 1971.

Dietmar Bruck epitomised the Sky Blue spirit in the 1960s. A hard-tackling defender who would play in any position for the cause. He made 217 appearances between 1961 and 1970 and his most memorable moment was scoring the equaliser in the 1963 FA Cup win over Sunderland.

Coventry-kid Bobby Gould broke into the first team in 1963 but only became a regular after Hudson left in 1966. By 1968 he was hot goalscoring property and Arsenal paid a record £90,000 for him. He went on to play for numerous clubs and returned to manage City in 1983.

Division 3 champions. Back row (left to right): G Hudson, R Wesson, J Sillett, J Hill (manager), D Meeson, M Kearns. Middle row: W Humphries, G Newton, G Curtis, G Kirby, J Mitten, R Rees. Front row: R Farmer, J Smith, H Barr, B Hill, E Machin, D Bruck. In March in a desperate attempt to check the slide, George Kirby was signed from Southampton for £12,500 and John Smith from Spurs for £11,000. It did the trick: Kirby scored a hat-trick on his home debut as Oldham were beaten 4-1 to end the barren run. George Hudson, a shadow of his former self for three months, was spurred into action and was recalled for the final game in which he became a legend by scoring the only goal.

December 1964. City's return to Division 2 started with a five-game winning sequence but by December they had slipped well down the table. After six games without a win and a humiliating 1-8 League Cup defeat at home to Leicester, manager Hill gambled on veteran Leicester striker Ken Keyworth. Keyworth scored on his debut against Rotherham but the defence, without the injured Curtis, fell apart and the visitors won 5-3. Here Hudson scores City's first goal.

July 1965. The club's whole staff of 81 pose for a unique picture. After a season's consolidation in Division 2 optimism was high, both in the club and in the city, that promotion to Division 1 was possible. The eagle-eyed reader may spot a walking stick behind Bill Glazier at the back of the group. He was recovering from a broken leg suffered at Maine Road in April, an injury which ended his hopes of being in England's 1966 World Cup squad.

September 1965. Manchester City under Joe Mercer and Malcolm Allison were the best side in the division but City gave them a fright at home, Manchester fortunate to get a point in a 3-3 draw. Here Hudson rifles home the third goal and his fifth in five games.

February 1966. Third placed City travel to Maine Road for the return against the league leaders. Johnny Crossan's second-minute goal is the winner for the home side in front of 40,190.

March 1966. Ron Farmer's penalty puts the Sky Blues on the road to a 3-1 home win over Cardiff and keeps the Sky Blues in the promotion race. Easter defeats at Portsmouth and Derby are their undoing, however, and Southampton snatch the second promotion place with City third, a point behind. Between 1962 and 1967 Farmer scored 21 goals from the penalty spot, missing only once, at Millwall in 1964.

August 1966. Chairman Derrick Robins pulls the first pint at the opening of the Sky Blue pub in Coundon. Jimmy Hill looks on and the smartly attired players are (left to right): Dietmar Bruck, John Tudor (partially hidden), George Curtis, Bobby Gould, Ray Pointer and Ron Farmer.

A product of City's youth scheme, Mick Coop made his first-team debut as a full-back during the 1966-67 season and over the next fifteen years made 488 appearances for the club. He later returned to coach the youth team to the FA Youth Cup in 1987.

October 1966. A shaky start to the season finds the Sky Blues back in eighth place but a 1-1 draw at second-placed Bolton is evidence that they are back in the promotion hunt. Curtis heads the ball clear, watched by John Tudor, Francis Lee, Ron Farmer and John Byrom. Ian Gibson has been dropped after a bust-up with Jimmy Hill but his return a month later sparked off a 25-match unbeaten run.

Christmas 1966. Jimmy Hill introduced an annual pop and crisps session for the young fans with the players providing the autographs. The players signing are (left to right): John Tudor, Bobby Gould, Bill Glazier, Ian Gibson, Dietmar Bruck (with cigarette), George Curtis (partially hidden) and Mick Kearns. The Sky Blues have just beaten Rotherham 4-2 to go second in the table.

March 1966. Bolton visit Highfield Road, as do the BBC Match of the Day cameras for the first time (the temporary TV gantry can be spotted at the rear of the Sky Blue stand). Gould raises his arms after scoring City's goal in the 1-1 draw and is about to be congratulated by Barry Lowes and Ernie Machin. The goal was created by Ronnie Rees with a dazzling 50-yard dribble and cross. City set a club record sixteen games unbeaten and now top the table.

John Key, a free transfer from Fulham the previous summer, scores the goal at Cardiff that virtually guarantees promotion. A 1-1 draw means that Blackburn had to win their three remaining games and City had to lose theirs. 5,000 City fans watch as Cardiff should have ended City's run but Toshack missed a penalty.

Wolves and City were both certain to be promoted but the season wasn't over. The fixture list had contrived an unforgettable climax, with the teams meeting in a game Hill tagged 'the Midlands Match of the Century' which would decide the championship. A record crowd of 51,455 squeezed into the ground with thousands of children lining the touchlines. Wolves led 1-0 at half-time but after the break City took control. Machin equalised and the crowd spilled on to the pitch. Gibson scored a brilliant second, again the crowd raced on and the referee threatened to postpone the game if it happened again. Rees (left) scored the third; the crowd dared not encroach until the final whistle when they engulfed their heroes, swarming in front of the main stand as Jimmy Hill led the singing of the Sky Blue song.

A draw at Ipswich and a 3-1 home win over Millwall on the final day clinched the title and the scenes in Coventry were memorable. An open-topped bus carried the team to Broadgate and on the balcony of the Hotel Leofric the trophy was presented amid wild scenes of celebration. Hill and Curtis (left) hold the trophy aloft. Below, City players record a special version of the Sky Blue Song with secretary Rose McNulty (later to become Sky Blue Rose on the club's special telephone line) adding vocals.

The full professional squad on the eve of the historic first ever season in Division 1. Little did anyone know that Jimmy Hill was in discussion about a new job in television. The news of his departure when it broke two days before the start of the new season rocked City fans. Line-up back row (left to right): P Denton, T Gould, R Hayward, D Peachey, D Roberts, M Clamp, A Dickie, W Glazier, J Blockley, M Coop, J Burckitt, B Lowes, P Morrissey.

Second row: D Bruck, B Glover, R Farmer, J Key, B Lewis, R Gould, M Kearns, G Curtis, J Tudor, B Hill, R Rees, I Gibson, E Machin, T Shepherd. Third row: P Hill (trainer), N Pilgrim (physiotherapist), A Leather (secretary), C Harrold (admin manager), Dr P Coghill (director), JR Mead (director), D Robins (Chairman), J Hill (manager), J Camkin (director), J Stevenson (director), A Dicks (assistant manager), P Saward (coach). Front row: I Crossley, T Sinclair, R Allen, G Paddon, R Dighton, D Icke, B Wilks, B Joy, W Carr, R Dobbing.

Chapter 7.

Two days before the club's baptism in the top flight Jimmy Hill announced that he was leaving the club to pursue a career in television. This was a blow which many people - inside and outside Coventry - thought would sound the death knell for the club's ambitions.

The first season in the top flight was long and hard and serious injuries to George Curtis and Ian Gibson made new manager Noel Cantwell's task all the harder. He spent over £300,000 on new players and, in what was a precursor for the future, the relegation battle went to the final game of the season. A goalless draw at the Dell kept City up. In its way, City's performances during 1967-68 were as heroic as any in the ensuing decades and it is testimony to the spirit of players and supporters alike that the average home gate of 34,715 has never been bettered.

By the end of February 1969 City had earned a miserly fourteen points from 25 games, but to general astonishment they yet again staged a dramatic recovery. City had to endure a tortuous wait as Leicester played out five outstanding fixtures, a product of inclement weather and a protracted FA Cup run, which carried Leicester to Wembley. They needed seven points to overhaul the Sky Blues' tally, but mustered just five, thereby finishing one point below Coventry. Rumours of favours for old friends circulated as Cantwell's former team, Manchester United, beat Leicester in their final game to save the Sky Blues.

No one would have predicted that twelve months later virtually the same team would finish sixth and qualify for Europe. The team's away form was the major reason for success with ten wins away from Highfield Road. In November the astute signings by Cantwell of Roy Barry and John O'Rourke helped consolidate a good start to the season and after a prodigious run of eight wins and a draw in ten games, City occupied fourth place. The place in Europe was clinched on a passionate night at Molineux when a Brian Joicey goal beat the old enemy.

Alas, the European experience was disappointing. After easily overcoming the Bulgarians, Trakia Plovdiv, City, without their injured keeper Glazier, slumped to a 1-6 defeat to Bayern Munich. The goals dried up and the season virtually ended in January when the club slumped out of the FA Cup at Rochdale.

In 1971-72 Cantwell was on trial from the start and by late autumn it looked as though City were in for what is euphemistically called a 'transitional season', but then things began to deteriorate. From early November until April, City mustered only one win in nineteen games, and after another FA Cup embarrassment, at home to Hull, Cantwell was sacked and caretaker manager Bob Dennison steered them to safety.

The first programme produced by the club in Division 1 for the game against Sheffield United in August 1967. The price had doubled to one shilling (5p) but the content was revolutionary and won the programme of the year award, the first of three successive titles. City's opening game at Burnley is featured on the cover and the signing of Tony Knapp as a replacement for Curtis has been too late for the printers to include in the line-up. City twice trail the Blades but goals from John Key and Dietmar Bruck earn a point.

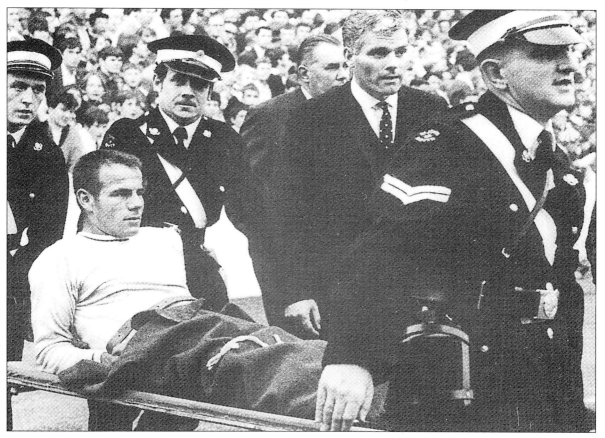

August 1967. Tragedy strikes in City's second game in Division 1. Captain courageous George Curtis breaks his leg in a collision with Forest's Frank Wignall. Jimmy Hill describes the 3-3 draw at the City Ground as the best performance in over 5 years. Curtis is out of action for eight months and his injury is one of many suffered by City's players that season.

September 1967. City's first visit to Stamford Bridge for 43 years ends in a 1-1 draw. Dave Clements scores the opening goal past Bonetti before Boyle equalises. Bill Glazier is the hero with a late penalty save from Charlie Cooke. City have only two wins from the first ten games.

14 October 1967. Noel Cantwell takes over as manager from Jimmy Hill who joins London Weekend Television. City put up a spirited display and come from two goals down to level, only for a Jimmy Greaves special to win it for the Londoners.

Boxing Day 1967. Liverpool visit Highfield Road for the first time and a crowd of over 42,000 see Scottish international Ian St John ordered off for striking City's Brian Lewis. A 1-1 draw leaves City at the foot of the table. Cantwell's autumnal signings Maurice Setters, Gerry Baker and Ernie Hannigan are settling in well and the defence looks far tighter with the warhorse Setters in it.

In February 1968 City faced Chelsea at Highfield Road with an all-Scottish forward line - (from left to right): Ernie Hannigan, signed from Preston for £55,000, Ian Gibson, Neil Martin, signed from Sunderland for £90,000, Gerry Baker, signed from Ipswich for £25,000, Willie Carr, homegrown. Baker, however, despite his Scottish accent, was born in New York, so is not strictly Scottish. Martin is making his debut as a replacement for Bobby Gould who has moved to Arsenal for £90,000. City beat Chelsea 2-1 with goals from Baker and Hannigan.

Arsenal visit Highfield Road and Glazier had a busy afternoon. Here he punches clear from Radford with Bruck and Clements providing cover. Gould scored for City but George Graham grabbed a late equaliser.

January 1968. In the FA Cup, City faced Third Division Tranmere Rovers at home. Ronnie Rees scored this goal, only for Rovers to grab a late equaliser. In the replay at Prenton Park the Sky Blues were humiliated 0-2 with former City legend George Hudson scoring one of the goals.

On 16 March 1968 the main stand was gutted by fire, leaving among the cinders a melted and twisted Second Division championship trophy and most of the club's archives. The stand was patched up sufficiently to enable the match of the season to go ahead ten days later. The opponents were European Champions-to-be Manchester United. A crowd of 47,111 witnessed a famous City victory, secured by goals from Ernie Machin and Maurice Setters.

The first-team squad for the 1968-69 season. Back row (left to right): D Clements, N Martin, D Bruck, M Setters, J Tudor, M Coop. Middle row: T Shepherd, B Hill, G Curtis, W Glazier, C Cattlin, J Blockley, M Kearns. Front row: E Hannigan, I Gibson, W Carr, N Cantwell, G Baker, E Hunt, E Machin.

Curtis is fit again but facing a tough battle for his place with both Setters and the youngster Blockley. Chris Cattlin and Ernie Hunt are the latest additions signed from Huddersfield and Everton respectively on the transfer deadline in March.

August 1968. From the ashes a new stand rises. Even though the new main stand was built in record time - the concrete construction was completed in 64 days - it was not ready for the start of the season and City kicked off a week late. The club had now constructed three new stands in four years and the ground was one of the most modern in the country.

September 1968. Ian Gibson is in a purple patch and the Sky Blues are unbeaten in four games. Here Gibbo scores the winner against Newcastle to lift City out of the bottom two, watched by John Tudor and Gerry Baker. From here, however, it is downhill and it is twelve games before City win again. There is another desperate fight against relegation.

May 1969. A week after surviving relegation by the skin of their teeth for the second successive season, City flew off to Barbados where they played three friendlies against local sides. Back (left to right): D Clements, N Martin, B Hill, W Carr, E Machin, T Shepherd, G Curtis, D Robins, P Robins, N Cantwell, N Pilgrim, M Coop. Front: J Blockley, M Setters, D Bruck, C Cattlin, E Hunt.

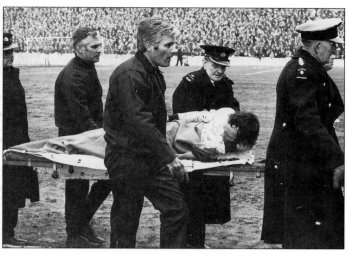

In October 1969 Noel Cantwell signed Roy Barry from Dunfermline for £40,000 and the gritty Scottish defender inspired an amazing run of results which took the club to the verge of Europe. He only played fourteen games before disaster struck and he broke his leg against Sheffield Wednesday. His injury kept him out for 14 months. Whilst he was a good defender for two seasons, he never scaled the heights of 1970 again.

September 1970. With a European Fairs Cup place guaranteed, Cantwell decided to strengthen the squad and paid Sheffield Wednesday a club record £100,000 for full-back Wilf Smith. Smith took time to settle but went on to make 151 appearances for the Sky Blues.

September 1970. City managed to hold Manchester United for almost an hour, then George Best scored. Five minutes later Glazier saves Best's free-kick but Bobby Charlton follows up to clinch the points. New boy Smith can do nothing to stop it.

City's first and only European campaign saw them drawn against Bulgarians Trakia Plovdiv in round one. John O'Rourke scores one of his three goals in the 4-1 first leg victory in Plovdiv. City won the second leg 2-0 to go through to round two, where they met the mighty Bayern Munich. The trip to Munich was a disaster. With Glazier injured, poor Eric McManus had a nightmare on a wet pitch and the Sky Blues lost 1-6. Two weeks later it was small compensation that City won the second leg 2-1. Their European odyssey was over.

October 1970. A visit to Elland Road in the early 1970s was a tough ordeal and City managed only two points from their first seven visits in the top flight. This season they were arguably at their peak and it was as good as over in the second minute when Geoff Strong's clearance cannoned off Glazier for an own-goal. City did keep the score down to 0-2. Blockley heads for goal with a young Dennis Mortimer admiring. Terry Cooper and Gary Sprake have things covered.

December 1970. It's ballet at Blackpool. City make their one and only top-flight visit to Bloomfield Road and in true Sky Blue fashion lose. Blackpool are arguably the worst side to play in the top flight during City's residency and won only four games all season. John Craven, later to sign for City, scored the winner. Dave Clements challenges Fred Kemp, whilst the veteran Jimmy Armfield looks on. City's other players are Geoff Strong and Neil Martin.

January 1971. City were drawn against Rochdale in the FA Cup third round. After a postponement caused by snow, manager Cantwell, in an unfortunate display of condescension, refused to play under Rochdale's candle-powered floodlights. When the game took place on a midweek afternoon, City were extinguished in one of the great cup humiliations. It was a watershed for the team, several of whom were soon out of the first-team frame. Dennis Butler scores the winning goal with Glazier and Carr helpless.

BBC's goal of the season and Coventry's goal of the century was the legendary 'donkey-kick' scored by Ernie Hunt who volleyed Willie Carr's deftly flicked free-kick over the Everton defensive wall and a bemused keeper. In this picture the pair are trying it again, before the FA banned it, against Tottenham. This time Hunt's shot thudded against the angle with Pat Jennings beaten.

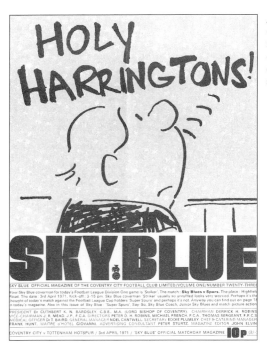

After three successive 'programme of the year' awards, City made radical changes with a company called Sportsgraphic producing a controversial magazine full of cartoons and unusual photographs. The fans loved or loathed it but after one season the club reverted to something more traditional.

September 1971. The famous green and black stripes get an airing at Stamford Bridge and City play their part in a 3-3 thriller. Billy 'Chips' Rafferty heads City's first goal, cancelling out Peter Osgood's goal. John O'Rourke watches in the knowledge that his Coventry career is almost over; City were on the verge of signing Chris Chilton from Hull City for £92,000. O'Rourke was sold to QPR within weeks. Chelsea defenders Ron Harris and David Webb can only stand and admire. Rafferty never established a regular place and signed for Blackpool in part-exchange for Tommy Hutchison just over a year later.

January 1972. The Sky Blues travel to St James' Park and lose a thriller 2-4. Malcolm Macdonald scored a penalty and City old boy John Tudor scored two. Earlier in the season City had lost 1-5 there in the Texaco Cup and the ground would prove to be a graveyard throughout the 1970s.

January 1972. Chris Chilton's finest moment in a Coventry shirt. He managed only four goals in 29 appearances before a back injury ended his career and this was the best. His header clinches a 2-1 FA Cup third round victory at the Hawthorns. Rafferty, following up, had scored the first goal. It is City's first away FA Cup win over a Division 1 side for 60 years.

January 1972. With normal penalty taker Ernie Hunt out injured, Jeff Blockley steps up to thunder the ball home past Ipswich's David Best in a 1-1 draw. Home gates have slipped below 17,000 though, and the pressure is building on manager Cantwell. FA Cup defeat at the hands of Hull City seal his fate after 41/2 years in charge.

Chapter 8.

The summer of 1972 saw the exciting appointment of Joe Mercer and Gordon Milne as managers of the club. Just weeks into the season the new team recognised the team's shortcomings and sold arguably the club's best asset, Jeff Blockley, to fund the purchase of Colin Stein and Tommy Hutchison, two of the most exciting players of the era. A good league run, three FA Cup wins and a high level of entertainment raised hopes, but Wolves shattered the Wembley dream in the quarter-finals and a miserable aftermath saw City slide to nineteenth place.

In 1973-74 the team flattered to deceive. The best ever start in the top flight was followed by a miserable six defeats in seven. The fans got excited in both Cup competitions before late defeats at QPR and Manchester City. In the summer of 1974, Milne believed he was one player short of a Championship challenging side - a centre-half. Deals were lined up to fund the purchase of Larry Lloyd for £240,000, but fell through after Lloyd signed. Suddenly, City were desperate for cash and with Derrick Robins and his money withdrawing from the board there was panic in the air. Over the next eighteen months many top players were sold to balance the books, several at knock-down prices and for many of the fans the last straw came at Christmas 1975, when star man Dennis Mortimer was sold to Aston Villa.

Jimmy Hill had returned as managing director in 1975, and later became chairman but failed to spark his magic a second time. After the Mortimer sale crowds dropped as low as 13,000 but the club were always in the safety of mid-table.

In 1976-77 after a poor start Milne made a number of shrewd signings including Terry Yorath and Ian Wallace. From looking very safe at Christmas a run of thirteen games without a win saw relegation once again staring them in the face. Speculation about Gordon Milne's future was rife and, coupled with a dreaded vote of confidence from Jimmy Hill, his future looked bleak. Hope resided largely in the newly established strikeforce of Ferguson and Wallace. Home victories over Derby and Stoke in April eased the situation, albeit temporarily, but two draws and two defeats left Coventry's First Division life hanging by a thread as they faced Bristol City at home in the final match of the season. The situation was finely balanced, with one or the other clearly favourites for the drop but in a night of high passion, Sunderland, not for the first time, were relegated whilst City survived by the skin of their teeth.

August 1972. New managers Joe Mercer and Gordon Milne vow to give the inherited squad a chance but the opening two games are lost, the second at Upton Park, courtesy of Clyde Best's header, which leaves Glazier and Coop beaten.

January 1973. Manchester United were in deep relegation trouble and Tommy Docherty's side, marshalled by big Jim Holton, defended grimly for a 1-1 draw. City, since the arrival of Colin Stein (pictured here) and Tommy Hutchison four months earlier, haven't lost at home. Bobby Charlton (number 9), looked out of place in a team of thugs, and can't stop Brian Alderson, out of picture, from scoring.

March 1973. Dreams of Wembley, inspired by comprehensive FA Cup victories over Orient, Grimsby and Hull City, are ended in the quarter-final at Molineux. John Richards scored an early goal and won the second-half penalty which Kenny Hibbitt slotted home to clinch it for Wolves. The defeat sparked a slump in league form that resulted in nine defeats in ten games.

September 1973. City started the new season with home wins over Tottenham and Liverpool and should have made it three out of three at Turf Moor. Paul Fletcher soars above the static John Craven (partially hidden) to put newly promoted Burnley ahead. Tommy Hutchison, Dennis Mortimer and Alan Dugdale watch. Two goals from livewire Alan Green makes the final score 2-2.

December 1973. The bare terraces at Old Trafford testify to Manchester United's worst season in years. David Cross, a recent £150,000 signing from Norwich, has just headed what turns out to be City's winning goal in a 3-2 victory. Less than 29,000 are at the 'Theatre of Dreams' to see George Best score what will be his last goal for the Reds. United are relegated.

December 1973. The Dell has always been a bogey ground for Coventry and a 1-1 draw meant it was 21 games without a win at Southampton. Mick Channon beats Glazier with a first-half penalty. City players watching are John Craven, Jim Holmes, Brian Alderson, Willie Carr and Alan Dugdale. Saints were fifth in the table but end the season being relegated after a disastrous run.

January 1974. In ten frenetic minutes at Maine Road, City's Wembley hopes go up in smoke. Leading Manchester City 2-1 in a League Cup quarter-final with twelve minutes left. Francis Lee, with two goals, and Denis Law break the Sky Blue hearts in a mudbath. Law, the poacher supreme, sweeps in the fourth past Craven and a grounded Glazier. The game was played on a midweek afternoon because of floodlight bans during the national power crisis.

April 1974. City are safe from relegation well before the end of season and won 1-0 in a grim game at Bramall Lane. The veteran Glazier, soon to be displaced, is on the floor as Craven heads clear. David Cross, a burly Peter Hindley, and Chris Cattlin watch.

October 1974. Graeme Souness shapes to shoot in a memorable 4-4 draw at Ayresome Park just after Middlesbrough, managed by Jack Charlton, won promotion. City had made their worst start for years but the point earned meant they were unbeaten in six and climbing up the league.

Coventry's Soccer Ball always attracted big names and in 1974 the new England manager Don Revie is the guest. He chats with City chairman Peter Robins and director Joe Mercer who had been a very successful caretaker manager of England prior to Revie's appointment.

February 1975. The record signing of centre-half Larry Lloyd from Liverpool the previous August had caused a financial crisis at the club and the sale of key players was necessary. A trip to Elland Road saw City recover from a midweek FA Cup defeat at Arsenal to earn a hard-fought 0-0 draw. Lloyd's form had been questionable and here he is beaten in the air by Gordon McQueen. City's players (in their change kit of red shirts with blue shorts) are (from left to right): Hindley (partially hidden), Lloyd, Hutchison, Alderson, Dugdale, Cattlin and Ramsbottom.

September 1975. New signing Barry Powell, who cost £75,000 from Wolves, is introduced to new colleagues Tommy Hutchison and Jim Blyth at the Ryton training ground. Manager Milne was given the go-ahead to sign Powell to consolidate a good start to the season. By December, however, with City in the bottom half of the table and the bank manager at the door, star midfielder Dennis Mortimer was controversially sold to Aston Villa for £175,000.

The mid-1970s were testing times for City fans with their stars sold to keep the club in the black but Tommy Hutchison was a constant source of pleasure during the period. He could always be relied upon to turn on a bit of magic to brighten up the dullest days. After joining City from Blackpool for £140,000 in 1972 he played 355 games for the club before joining Manchester City in 1980.

The 1975-76 season was memorable for centre-forward David Cross. He scored two hat-tricks, both away from home, one on the first day of the season, the other on the last day, at Everton and Burnley respectively. His strength was in the air and he scored 36 goals in 106 games before joining West Brom in 1976. Later he had five good years at West Ham.

The 1976-77 season started badly for the Sky Blues and three shrewd purchases Bobby McDonald (above), Terry Yorath and Ian Wallace, put things back on track. Scots-born McDonald, a true left footer with a penchant for overlapping, made 178 consecutive appearances as City's left-back before joining Manchester City in 1980.

The true extent of the club's ambitions were laid bare in December 1975 when Dennis Mortimer, an outstanding midfielder, was sold to Aston Villa. His powerful runs from midfield allied to his composure on the ball had won him six Under-23 caps but sadly he never won the full cap he deserved. He did however lift the European Cup as captain of Villa's successful team in 1982.

Ipswich Town's David Johnson is surrounded by City defenders but still manages to get a shot in. City won a rare point at Portman Road where Bobby Robson built a succession of good teams in the 1970s. Pictured are John Craven, Jim Holmes and Jim Brogan. The veteran Brogan, a Scottish international, joined on a free transfer from Celtic in 1975 and gave excellent value for one season.

John Craven was not the most delicate midfielder of his era but here he is pictured taking on the Leeds United defence with a hint of a body swerve, watched by Terry Yorath, the man who would replace him at Highfield Road a few months later. A former team-mate of Gordon Milne at Blackpool, Craven was a competitive player who never gave less than 100%.

January 1977. City won 1-0 away to bottom of the table Sunderland on a bitterly cold night on a rock-hard pitch. Donal Murphy's 90th-minute goal put City in 11th place. The goal turned out to be vital; four months later the Sky Blues would avoid relegation by virtue of finishing one point ahead of relegated Sunderland. Jim Blyth catches confidently, watched by Coop and Dugdale.

January 1977. Alan Dugdale's clearing header is deflected off Lou Macari for the first goal in City's 0-2 defeat at Old Trafford. It was the start of a depressing run of one win in 16 games for the Sky Blues.

March 1977. A new team photo taken to coincide with the arrival of Jim Holton from Sunderland for £40,000. Back row (left to right): B Roberts, L Cartwright, M Coop, R McDonald, D Murphy, J Beck. Middle row: T Yorath, T Hutchison, J Blyth, B King, J Holton, M Ferguson, A Dugdale. Front row: A Green, I Wallace, G Milne (manager), R Wylie (coach), G Oakey, B Powell. By this time Bryan King, a £57,000 signing from Millwall in 1975, had played his final game and would be forced to retire through injury soon afterwards.

March 1977. Another away defeat, this time 1-3 at St Andrews, sees City slide a little closer to the relegation zone. Jim Blyth (right) has been drawn out of position by man of the match Trevor Francis who scores the opening goal from an acute angle. Yorath, McDonald and Holmes are helpless. An Easter injury to Blyth meant a call-up for 19-year-old Les Sealey, who shone in the last eleven games.

May 1977. The vital relegation game with Bristol City. Hutchison puts City ahead in a game delayed for fifteen minutes because of traffic problems. City lost a 0-2 lead and with ten minutes left were hanging on at 2-2 when news came through that Sunderland had lost at Everton and if the score remained at 2-2 both City and Bristol were safe. A truce is called and Bristol players pass the ball amongst themselves.

Chapter 9.

Few who had seen City survive by the skin of their teeth in the previous season could have predicted that the Sky Blues would have arguably their best ever season in the top flight in 1977-78. They missed out on Europe by a whisker and produced some of the finest home displays seen for years. The Ian Wallace-Mick Ferguson partnership blossomed, a settled side was possible and the team scored 75 league goals. Everything clicked and manager Milne, under severe pressure just months earlier, was suddenly the attacking football guru.

The following season was inevitably a disappointment, despite a top-half finish in the League. Injuries to Yorath and Ferguson meant the fans' high expectations were not achieved but the team again had an outstanding home record and Wallace scored more great goals. Away from home things went sour after two early wins. At West Brom in October the team, playing in their infamous chocolate brown shirts, melted under the heat of Ron Atkinson's exciting team, and suffered the club's biggest defeat since 1958. Then in December there were successive heavy defeats at Southampton and Bristol City. After another walloping at the Hawthorns in the FA Cup, Milne tightened up the defence and the season ended with City as the draw specialists.

The inconsistencies continued the following season and were exemplified by successive games in January. The first a well-deserved home win over the champions Liverpool, the second an ignominious FA Cup defeat at Third Division Blackburn. The fact that a new batch of excellent home-grown players was emerging did nothing to reduce the inevitable pressure on the long-serving Milne. He survived despite results and a questionable transfer policy that had seen relatively big buys such as Gary Collier, David Jones and Roger Van Gool fail.

Jimmy Hill took over as chairman in the summer of 1980 and almost his first act was to sell Ian Wallace for a record £1.25 million. The cynics said the £1.25 million had to fund the new Sky Blue Connexion at Ryton, and when just weeks into the season the experienced Tommy Hutchison and Bobby McDonald were also sold the fans were grumbling. Milne gambled all on his kids and it paid off with a stirring League Cup run with the club reaching the semi-final for the first time, only to lose to West Ham over two legs. However the youngsters tired and sixteenth position was deemed not good enough. Milne was not to get another chance and was moved 'sideways' to general manager as Dave Sexton arrived as team manager.

September 1977. The Sky Blues started the new season well and a 2-1 win at Newcastle, their first there since 1939, puts them 5th in the table. Ian Wallace (here scoring the first goal) had scored seven goals in seven games and his striking partnership with Mick Ferguson is paying off. City players (left to right): Graydon, Wallace, McDonald and Ferguson.

February 1978. City travelled to the Hawthorns for a vital game as both clubs pushed for a European place. The honours are even with Ron Atkinson's attractive team in a 3-3 draw. Brian Roberts chases Albion's Scottish international winger, Willie Johnston, for the ball.

April 1978. City faced Bristol City in the last match of the season again, this time it's at Ashton Gate and City need a win to make a European place certain. Here Joe Royle puts Bristol ahead, with Blyth, McDonald and Osgood helpless. A minute later Ian Wallace's 23rd goal of the season levelled matters but a 1-1 draw leaves them relying on Arsenal winning the FA Cup. The Gunners, however, lose to Ipswich and Europe is still a dream.

Ray Graydon joined Coventry on a free transfer in the summer of 1977. The goalscoring right-winger played only 17 games for the club but created a hatful of chances for the deadly goalscoring partnership of Ian Wallace and Mick Ferguson and scored six goals of his own, including the winner in the memorable 5-4 win over Norwich at Christmas.

In 1977-78 season City scored 75 league goals, far and away the biggest haul in their top-flight history. Ian Wallace and Mick Ferguson scored 38 between them and the total would have been more but for 'Fergie' missing 12 games through injury. Wallace deservedly won Scottish international honours, but amazingly didn't make the 1978 World Cup party. Ferguson was touted as a possible England striker but never got the call. The photograph on the programme cover was from the previous season when Wallace scored a hat-trick against Peter Shilton, a very rare feat.

Three Scottish internationals pose for the camera. (Left to right): Tommy Hutchison, Jim Blyth and Jim Holton. Hutchison won 17 caps between 1973 and 1975 and probably deserved more. Blyth was capped twice in 1978 and was in that year's World Cup party in Argentina but was never selected again. Holton won 15 caps before he joined City. In late 1978 Blyth's proposed £440,000 transfer to Manchester United fell through when he failed the medical. Holton sadly died in 1993 whilst running a pub in Coventry.

July 1978. It's photo call again and Ferguson, Wallace and Yorath relax between poses. City again started the season well and despite rarely being out of the top half of the table there wasn't the same buzz as the previous year.

'Don't forget to put the milk bottles out, Fergie,' says Tommy Hutchison. A scene from the cafeteria at the Ryton training ground. In the background are (left to right): Jim Holton, Bill Trew, the boot man, John Beck and Donato Nardiello.

October 1978. The only addition to the squad was Steve Hunt, a former Aston Villa winger who had made his name with New York Cosmos and was snapped up by Gordon Milne for £40,000. He scored on his debut at Derby but at West Brom a few weeks later he couldn't save the City from an embarrassing 1-7 defeat. The infamous chocolate brown shirts didn't bring City much luck. Barry Powell is the other Coventry player.

November 1978. Ian Wallace is closely marked by Arsenal's Irish international Pat Rice during the 1-1 draw at Highfield Road. Wallace suffered from the absence of his partner Ferguson, injured for over half of the season, but still managed 15 goals.

July 1979. Two new signings for the new season. Gary Collier (left) a centre-back who was the first English player to exercise his right to leave at the end of his contract when he left Bristol City for £325,000. David Jones (right) another centre-back who cost £250,000 from Everton. Neither player was able to force their way into the first team: Collier was sold to Portland Timbers a year later, whilst Jones moved to Hong Kong.

December 1979. Injuries have hindered City's progress but when Ferguson and Wallace are together they are unbeatable. A 4-1 victory over Ipswich makes it four games unbeaten but more importantly Ferguson scores all four goals against the team who a week earlier offered a derisory £750,000. Here he takes on Ipswich's Terry Butcher.

Gordon Milne's first foreign signing was Roger Van Gool who cost £250,000 from Cologne in February 1980. The Belgian international winger was a great disappointment and played only 19 games. His arrival coincided with a transfer request from Ian Wallace which was ultimately granted and led to a £1.25 million transfer to Nottingham Forest.

The sales of Wallace, Hutchison and McDonald in 1980 enabled a number of outstanding young players to become regulars in the first team. Amongst them were forwards Tom English and Gary Thompson, pictured here. Thompson ended 1980-81 as top scorer with 15 goals.

November 1980. Prince Philip officially opens the Sky Blue Connexion, a sports complex at Ryton, doubling as the club's training ground. Cynical fans described it as the 'Wallace Connexion', implying that it was paid for with the Wallace transfer money. Left to right: Tom Sergeant (director), Gordon Milne (manager), Jimmy Hill (chairman), Prince Philip.

City's exciting League Cup run took them to a two leg semi-final with West Ham. In a remarkable first leg they came from two goals down to win 3-2. Above, Alvin Martin tackles Andy Blair. Below, West Ham's Alan Devonshire watches the ball roll into Coventry's net after confusion between Les Sealey (left) and Garry Thompson caused the young striker to score an own-goal.

Coventry's team of kids celebrate a 5-0 home League Cup replay victory over Watford. Victories over Manchester United, Brighton and Cambridge United took them through to the quarter-finals. The average age is under 21, the youngest side in the club's history. Back (left to right): Danny Thomas, Brian Roberts, Andy Blair. Front: Peter Bodak, Paul Dyson, Gary Gillespie, Garry Thompson, Les Sealey, Steve Hunt, Mark Hateley, Gerry Daly.

Chapter 10.

Dave Sexton's arrival in 1981 coincided with the transformation of Highfield Road into an all-seater stadium with a capacity reduced from 36,000 to 20,500. The whole Hill-inspired project, however, only increased the fans' disillusionment with the club. There had been no consultation with them about the major changes and with on-field performances dipping the average gates slumped to 13,000. The club not only invested more money in the doomed USA league but also continued to sell good players without replacing them.

Safety was achieved in Sexton's first season with a good end-of-season run, but with no new signings, matters did not improve the following campaign. Attendances fell to 8,000 and the club was losing money at a serious rate.

In February 1983 Garry Thompson became the latest sacrifice when he was sold to West Brom. This sale by Jimmy Hill, against the will of Sexton, sparked off a chain of events which saw City go thirteen games without a win, yet avoid relegation by the skin of their teeth. Hill was forced off the board, Sexton was sacked on the last day of the season, and eight first team players rejected new contracts and left Highfield Road.

New manager Bobby Gould had the onerous task of putting together a side from scratch for the 1983-84 season but his experience of the lower divisions enabled him to snap up some real bargains, many of whom were still at the club when City reached Wembley four years later.

Despite being fourth in the table at Christmas things went drastically wrong in 1984 and the final day of the season arrived with a win needed to survive relegation. By Christmas 1984 City were 21st in the table and Gould was sacked by new chairman John Poynton.

His caretaker successor was Don Mackay, who steered them to safety by virtue of winning the final three games of the season, including a nail-biting finale against the champions Everton.

Once again City were in deep financial trouble with debts of over £1 million but despite a lot of promise in 1985-86 they were left needing to win their final game to survive, for the third successive season. Mackay resigned with three games left and George Curtis and John Sillett took over, clinched safety and promised a new approach.

Many fans were cynical and few would have guessed that the new approach, a bold attacking style, would result in the club winning the FA Cup just twelve months later. The early season form was good and the team were rarely out of the top eight. The real excitement, however, came in a thrilling FA Cup run which culminated in one of the finest finals seen at Wembley with City deservedly beating Spurs 3-2 after extra-time.

The summer of 1981 saw Highfield Road become the first all-seater stadium in England. Seats were installed on terrace areas but only ten rows were installed on the Kop. The capacity was reduced from 36,000 to 21,000 and the average gate plummeted by 25% to 13,000. The fans were unhappy that every game was made all-ticket and felt alienated by the hurried and tactless manner in which the ground had been converted. Within two years the standing area at the rear of the Kop was reopened and in 1985 all the Kop seats were removed. That same summer of 1981 saw Gordon Milne moved upstairs after nine years in charge and replaced by former Chelsea and Manchester United manager Dave Sexton.

Gerry Daly was the experienced Eire international who helped City's young team during the early 1980s. Purchased from Derby County in 1980 he didn't last long in the Sexton era; the new boss bought his old captain from QPR Gerry Francis and froze Daly out. After helping Leicester City to promotion whilst on loan in 1983 he made a return under Bobby Gould.

The 1981-82 season was uninspiring apart from an amazing 13-match run with only one defeat which took City out of a seemingly impossible position in early March. Les Sealey, recalled after spending the season in the reserves, kept seven clean sheets in nine games to win a trophy presented by a national newspaper.

November 1982. An already strained relationship between the club and the Coventry Evening Telegraph was exacerbated with an editorial criticising the club, and chairman Jimmy Hill in particular, for being out of touch with the fans. Storm clouds were hovering above Highfield Road and before the end of the season changes would be made.

August 1982. The full professional squad line up in their Talbot shirts. Sexton was given no money to spend and the fans voted with their feet; only 10,000 turned up for the first home game. Back row (left to right): S Whitton, G Thompson, P Dyson, J Blyth, L Sealey, M Hateley, G Gillespie, I Butterworth, S Jacobs. Second row: C Dobson (reserve team coach), G Dalton (trainer), G Daly, M McGinty, L McGrath, T Dalton, P Suckling, J Matthews, M Conroy, B Edwards (youth recruitment manager), J Sillett (chief scout). Third row: T English, M Singleton, J Hendrie, B Roberts, D Sexton (manager), G Francis, S Mardenborough, D Thomas, P Hormantschuk. Front row: N Bollard, K Thompson, unknown, D Hall, A Spring, J McDonald.

The one bright spot on the increasingly dull horizon was the consistent form of City right-back Danny Thomas. In November he won a call-up to the England full squad after several outstanding performances for the Under 21s and was chosen as the Young Player of the month. Six months later he would deservedly become City's first England cap since Reg Matthews. Sadly within weeks he had left the club to join Tottenham.

Brian Roberts, nicknamed 'Harry' by colleagues and fans, was a consistent performer during the early 1980s and was one of few first-team players who stayed after the summer of discontent of 1983, becoming Bobby Gould's captain. In December 1982 he scored his first ever goal, after 192 appearances, prompting fans to produce badges made with the words 'I saw Harry score'. Within a few weeks he did it again, in an FA Cup-tie with Norwich.

February 1983. The spark that starts the 1983 revolution. Garry Thompson was sold to West Brom for £225,000 to 'balance the books' and Sexton was unhappy with being left with only fourteen senior players. Thompson teamed up with Cyrille Regis, who ironically would join the Sky Blues eighteen months later. The club was in turmoil, the team went from outside bets for Europe to dead-certs for relegation with a 13-game run without a win and the fans were at the end of their tether. The board acted and Hill was ousted, relegation was avoided and Bobby Gould lined up to succeed Sexton. Almost half the squad's contracts expired and they all opted to depart; a great young side was decimated.

November 1983. There are thirteen new players in the team photo. The latest signing is Stuart Pearce, a £25,000 snip from Wealdstone. The team, put together by Gould on a shoestring budget, has had a remarkable start to the season and are in the top six, on merit. Back row (left to right): S Jacobs, I Butterworth, G Withey, D Bamber, S Allardyce, A Grimes, T Peake, P Hormantschuk. Middle row: B Edwards (youth recruitment manager), B Eastick (youth team coach), E Kelly, J Matthews, S Pearce, T Dalton, R Avramovic, P Suckling, N Platnauer, D Hall, D Bennett, J Sillett (coach), G Dalton (trainer). Front row: M Singleton, M Adams, T Gibson, B Roberts, R Gould (manager), J Hendrie, M Gynn, S Hunt, L McGrath.

December 1983. The most remarkable result of a remarkable season. City hammered champions Liverpool 4-0, with Terry Gibson scoring the first of his hat-trick. The win takes the Sky Blues to fourth in the table. Mark Lawrenson and Phil Neal are spectators, as are City players Platnauer and Bamber.

January 1984. City start the New Year with a 2-1 home win over Sunderland on a waterlogged pitch. It would be City's last league win until April as a 13-game run without a win sends them spiralling down the table towards relegation. Steve Jacobs wins the ball supported by Ashley Grimes. Grimes, the former Manchester United midfielder, was a major disappointment and was sold to Luton at the end of the season.

May 1984. A 'must win' game against Luton Town as relegation looms. Eleven minutes from time Terry Gibson nets his 19th goal of the season to grab a point. Stuart Pearce is following up. The poor crowd of 9,647 seems to indicate that the fans don't care if they are relegated.

Coventry players Michael Gynn, Brian Roberts, Nicky Platnauer and Graham Withey escape from the relegation worries by opening the Rose Inn.

March 1984. The bad run continued as a crushing 1-4 home defeat against Arsenal leaves the Sky Blues only four points off the drop zone. City can't beat the Gunners despite going ahead, playing against ten men and against a side who played the last half hour with Stewart Robson in goal for the injured Jennings. Here Jennings dives at Gibson's feet whilst Chris Whyte, later to be ordered off, blocks Dave Bennett.

Manager Bobby Gould and Chairman Ian Jamieson celebrate as Norwich are beaten 2-1 on the final day of the season and City are safe. Birmingham who drew 0-0 with Southampton are relegated. Mick Ferguson, back on loan (from Birmingham!) equalised the Canaries' early penalty, and Dave Bennett scored the winner direct from a corner, twenty minutes from time. At that stage either a Norwich equaliser or a Birmingham goal at St Andrews would have sent City down. Four minutes from time Norwich's Robert Rosario headed against the bar but City held out.

July 1984. Six new faces for the new season including former England striker Bob Latchford and £72,000 goalkeeper Steve Ogrizovic. Back row (left to right): T Peake, M Jol, S Ogrizovic, B Kilcline, P Suckling, G Withey, I Butterworth. Middle row: K Stephens, S Pearce, N Platnauer, R Latchford, A Spring, K Hibbitt, D Bennett, P Hormantschuk. Front row: K Thompson, T Gibson, M Adams, R Gould (manager), M Gynn, M Singleton, L McGrath.

October 1984. The new season is depressingly familiar. One win out of the first eight games found them in the bottom three throughout the autumn and Gould responded by buying two star-names: Cyrille Regis, £300,000 from West Brom, and Peter Barnes, £65,000 from Leeds. Neither player had a good start for the Sky Blues and after a Boxing Day defeat at Luton Gould is sacked and replaced by his number 2, Don Mackay. At Chelsea in November (right) City lead 2-0, only to capitulate in the second half and lose 2-6.

January 1985. Gibson scores the first of two goals that knock Manchester City out of the FA Cup on a frozen pitch. It is a welcome relief from the league struggle but they lose in the fourth round at Old Trafford after Gibson misses a penalty.

May 1985. The City players faces tell the story at Portman Road. A 0-0 draw means that the Sky Blues have to win their last three games in order to stay up. Amazingly they win at Stoke and beat Luton and champions Everton to overtake Norwich and avoid relegation. It is the first time in two years that they have won three back-to-back games.

Everton may be without four of their regulars but they are no match for a rampant Sky Blues who win 4-1. Regis with two, Adams and Gibson, here scoring the fourth, are City's scorers. A crowd of 21,596, the largest since the ground capacity was reduced in 1981, cannot believe their eyes.

Messrs Bennett, Hibbitt and Peake take a break from the rigours of fighting relegation to visit a local factory.

1985-86 season and the new £80,000 full-back Brian Borrows made his debut after his move from Bolton. Borrows went on to make 487 appearances for the club and was unlucky not to play for England. Behind him are Michael Gynn and David Bowman, a midfield player signed from Hearts for £165,000 the previous season. Bowman started well but found the pressures of a relegation scrap too much and returned to Scotland after 30-odd games. City started the season poorly but after a mini-revival in October kept their head above the relegation waves for most of the campaign.

(Left to right): Don Mackay (manager), Ted Stocker (vice-chairman), Steve Ogrizovic, Trevor Peake and Brian Kilcline. These three players, all Gould signings, formed the core of the defence for seven years and made over 1,100 appearances for the club. Centre-half Kilcline arrived in 1984 with a hard-man reputation but received only one red card in his time at Coventry.

September 1985. City notch their first win of the season, 5-2 against Division newcomers Oxford United. Bennett lashes home the first goal and former-Sky Blue Bobby McDonald can't stop it. McDonald did score twice on his return to the ground. Gibson and Gynn are in the background.

October 1985. Ray Clemence just fails to stop Kilcline's penalty that puts City 2-1 ahead against Spurs. The Londoners came back to win 3-2, a rare win over the Sky Blues in the 1980s which saw City become their bogey side. Messrs Roberts, Ardiles, Hoddle and Stevens watch.

November 1985. City won 2-0 on the plastic pitch at QPR, two weeks after becoming the first side to win on Luton's artificial turf. Goals from the ubiquitous Gibson, by this time coveted by several big clubs, and a Byrne own-goal sealed the points. The away end is conspicuously empty; City's away followings rarely numbered more than a few hundred during the season. Here Adams shoots for goal.

May 1986. The return with QPR is the final game of the season and after their annual spring slump the Sky Blues again need to win to stay up. George Curtis and John Sillett replaced Don Mackay with three games left and their influence is just enough. After QPR have taken the lead Kilcline's rocket free-kick thunders into the net. Seven minutes later Bennett coolly slots home the winner.

Terry Gibson set a new club Division 1 scoring record by netting in seven successive games in the autumn of 1985. Why he is holding a number 8 shirt with eight balls is a mystery. In January, City found Manchester United's £650,000 offer too much to refuse and after 52 goals in 113 games he moved to Old Trafford. The proceeds were spent on three players, Nick Pickering, Alan Brazil and Jim McInally, only one of whom, Pickering, would survive to the next season.

January 1987. Managers Curtis and Sillett had the Sky Blues playing some exciting, attacking soccer and they were never out of the top half of the table. The third round of the FA Cup brought Bolton to town and on a freezing pitch they are sent packing 3-0 and Regis scored the second goal. After two inconsistent seasons, Regis is in wonderful form as the team at last play to his strengths.

A 1-0 fourth round win at Old Trafford, courtesy of Keith Houchen's scrambled goal, sparks Cup fever in Coventry. New United boss Alex Ferguson blames the icy pitch!

It's away to Stoke! City's players listen to the fifth round draw at Ryton. (Left to right): Ogrizovic, Peake, Pickering, Emerson, Phillips (partially hidden), McGrath, Houchen, Kilcline, Bennett and Regis. Dean Emerson, a £40,000 signing from Rotherham, has been inspirational in midfield but would miss out on Wembley after suffering a serious knee injury.

A Michael Gynn goal is enough to beat Stoke City at the Victoria Ground and Greg Downs salutes the large travelling support who now believe that City's name is on the cup. Ogrizovic, Borrows and Phillips are in the background.

Messrs Curtis and Sillett receive the Bells Manager of the Month award for April 1987, recognition of their achievement in taking the Sky Blues to their first Wembley final.

A tough trip to Hillsborough in the quarter-finals is successfully overcome. Regis roared away to score one of his trademark goals and put City ahead. 15,000 City fans are packed into the infamous Leppings Lane end.

Keith Houchen, nicknamed 'Roy of the Rovers', grabbed two late goals to clinch a semi-final place. Here he steers the ball home with Bennett in attendance. City were drawn to meet Leeds United in the semi-final and it meant a return to Hillsborough.

Bennett and Regis celebrate reaching Wembley after a famous 3-2 extra-time victory over Leeds. City trailed for almost an hour, then goals from Gynn and Houchen gave them the advantage. A late Edwards equaliser took the game into an extra half hour but Dave Bennett clinched the final place in the 99th minute.

Kilcline, Gynn and Bennett are exhausted but ecstatic after the semi-final victory. For Bennett it would be his third trip to Wembley, having played in Manchester City's side in the replayed 1981 final, against Tottenham.

The first day cover tells the story of the 1987 FA Cup final. Tottenham, the odds-on favourites, are beaten in a Wembley FA Cup final for the first time in eight visits.

A proud John Sillett leads the team out at Wembley on 16 May 1987. Sillett's Tottenham counterpart, David Pleat, is out of the picture but captain Richard Gough is visible. Tottenham's fans are situated at the tunnel end in the background.

Clive Allen had put Spurs ahead in the second minute but seven minutes later City were level as Houchen flicked on Greg Downs' free-kick and Bennett was in like a flash to score.

Kilcline holds the trophy aloft and City are the winners. Gary Mabbutt had put Spurs 2-1 ahead, Houchen equalised with his famous diving header and Mabbutt's extra-time own-goal from Lloyd McGrath's cross proved to be the winner. The trophy has been presented by the Duchess of Kent on whose right, leading the applause, is chairman John Poynton.

The famous trophy adorned with sky blue ribbons for the first time in the club's 104-year history.

142

The team celebrate in front of the massed ranks of their supporters. Back row (left to right): Regis, Gynn, Houchen, McGrath, Peake, Kilcline, Sedgley, Bennett, unknown fan. Front row: Phillips, Ogrizovic, Pickering, Rodger, Downs. Sedgley and Rodger were the substitutes. Graham Rodger came on for the injured Kilcline at the end of normal play whilst Sedgley remained on the bench.

Chapter 11.

The period since the 1987 Cup triumph can be divided into three distinct eras. Firstly the Sillett years from 1987 until his poorly handled departure in October 1990. During this time the Sky Blues were never in relegation trouble and finished in comfortable mid-table. Shock Cup defeats, however, were the order of the day, including severe embarrassments at Sutton in 1989 and Northampton in 1990. The Wembley heroes formed the basis of the side for the whole of the period with the only major acquisition being David Speedie, purchased in the summer of 1987 with the proceeds of the cup run.

This era was followed by an unsatisfactory four and half years when the club had four managers and a similarly rapid turnover of playing staff. Terry Butcher, an experienced player but an inexperienced manager, succeeded Sillett but was woefully out of his depth and lasted little more than a year. Once Peter Robins returned as chairman, replacing John Poynton who had become somewhat complacent, the writing was on the wall for Butcher. He was unhappy at a reduction in his salary when he retired from playing and the club later lost a High Court case over the issue. Don Howe stepped into the breach as caretaker in January 1992 and in one of the most depressing seasons in the club's modern history almost managed to get the club relegated. It took a late goal by Notts County to send Luton down whilst a spineless City lost at Villa Park.

Bobby Gould returned that summer and once again made a silk purse out of a pig's ear. Not only were Coventry the first ever leaders of the new Premier League but they were still in the top six in March and a final position of fifteenth gave a false impression. The following season, with Bryan Richardson now in the chair, started equally promisingly but in October Gould's shock resignation pushed his assistant, Phil Neal into the limelight. A good end-of-season run saw the team finish eleventh but the fans were not convinced about Neal and after a dreadful run in the winter of 1994 he was sacked as the club teetered just above the relegation abyss.

In stepped Ron Atkinson to start the third and final era of the post-Wembley period. Ron and his new assistant Gordon Strachan kept the team up in 1995 and again in 1996, though on both occasions there was too little room for comfort. In November 1996, with a third successive relegation battle looming, Strachan took over. His scrape with relegation that season saw City go closer than they had ever gone to the edge.

In 1997-98 City had their best season for years, finishing eleventh in a very competitive league and reaching the quarter-finals of the FA Cup, but they were unable to build on that foundation in the following two seasons. As the first full season of the 21st century commenced, a new chapter in the club's fascinating history began with City's prodigious young striker, Robbie Keane, joining Internazionale of Milan in a £13 million deal.

Season ticket sales rocketed in the run up to the FA Cup final in 1987 as fans took the opportunity of buying for the new season and guaranteeing a Wembley ticket. In August 1987 City had over 8,500 season ticket holders compared to under 3,000 a year previously. The attractive new kit created by Hummel was almost a throwback to the 1960s. Here is Cyrille Regis, whose performances in 1987-88 earned him a recall to the England squad and a cap to add to the four he had won at West Brom.

August 1988. Brian Kilcline thunders a penalty towards Everton's Neville Southall. The vicious shot beat Neville but hit the bar and the Blues won 1-0. It was a rare miss for 'Killer', although he failed from the spot later in the season against champions-elect Arsenal, only to redeem himself later in the game when City were awarded a second penalty by scoring the winner.

October 1988. Steve Sedgley has become a regular in the side playing as the midfield destroyer. Here he beats Millwall's aggressive midfielder Terry Hurlock to the ball as he goes for goal. Newly promoted Millwall won a hard-earned point in a 0-0 draw. Sedgley got his dream move to Tottenham the following summer.

November 1988. After 51 years and 26 league meetings, the old enemy Aston Villa are beaten at last. After Regis had scored an early goal Houchen scored the second and manager Sillett describes the team as 'the best Coventry side ever'. It would be the last goal Houchen scored for the Sky Blues; in March 1989 he signed for Hibernian.

January 1989. David Speedie was purchased with the profits from the 1987 Cup run and cost £780,000 from Chelsea. He was a popular player at Highfield Road, even though he wasn't the prolific scorer City needed. Here he heads one of a hat-trick of headers in a 5-0 thumping of Sheffield Wednesday. Five days later the Sky Blues, with eight of the Wembley heroes on show, were inexplicably dumped out of the FA Cup by non-league Sutton United. John Sillett didn't heed the warning signs however and continued to support the old guard.

October 1989. In an effort to pep up an attack that did not score enough goals, John Sillett paid Glasgow Rangers £800,000 for Kevin Drinkell. Despite an impressive scoring record in Scotland, he was past his best and it was a disastrous buy. He spent eighteen months in the reserves before his contract was terminated.

October 1990. After a second successive Cup embarrassment, this time at Northampton, Sillett's days were numbered. His departure however was badly handled by chairman Poynton and his replacement, Terry Butcher, was installed with almost obscene haste. Butcher was given a player-manager's contract and also cost a £400,000 transfer fee. He would play only seven games for the club before being forced to retire through injury. At that point his dual contract became a bone of contention. Here he runs out for his debut at home to Liverpool which City unluckily lost 0-1.

Butcher's first match in charge and City give the Liverpool defence a hard time. Pictured left to right are: Brian Borrows, Lloyd McGrath, Michael Gynn, Gary Gillespie (partially hidden), David Burrows, Gary Ablett (number 10).

November 1990. City's first victory under Butcher and a memorable Rumbelows Cup victory over Nottingham Forest who have won the trophy for the last two years. Kevin Gallacher scores the first goal of his first-half hat-trick and City led 4-0 after 35 minutes. A seven-minute hat-trick from Nigel Clough and another from Parker makes it 4-4 until Steve Livingstone snatches the winner. Gallacher wheels away in celebration with City's other players (from left to right): Livingstone, Regis and Speedie. Clough and former City favourite Stuart Pearce can't believe it.

Livingstone makes it 3-0 with David Smith waiting to make sure.

July 1991. Butcher's team line-up for a photo call. Back row (left to right): M Gynn, S Robson, T Peake, R Rosario, A Pearce, P Billing, P Ndlovu, L Middleton. Middle row: G Dalton (trainer), B Borrows, L Hurst, S Ogrizovic, P Edwards, L McGrath, B Eastick (reserve team coach), M Mills (coach). Front row: K Sansom, R Woods, K Drinkell, T Butcher (player-manager), D Smith, D Emerson, K Gallacher. In the summer of 1991 Butcher freed Regis and sold Kilcline to Oldham. Speedie had gone to Liverpool in the previous February and Peake fell out with Butcher and was sold a week into the season.

May 1992. At the end of a depressing season which saw Butcher sacked in January after 14 months in charge, and his successor Don Howe bored the fans senseless, Stewart Robson received the player of the year award from the London Supporters Club. Robson had joined the club in the previous summer on a free transfer and his tigerish midfield play won the fans over. Injuries restricted his appearances to 14 games the following season and in 1994 he was forced to retire.

August 1992. The new Premier League kicks off and new manager Bobby Gould's first signing, John Williams, scores against Middlesbrough after 12 minutes. The Sky Blues won their first three games to become the first ever leaders of the new league.

August 1992. Blackburn Rovers, back in the top division thanks to the money of Jack Walker, grabbed a 2-0 win at Coventry. Lee Hurst, City's brightest home-grown talent for years, shoots just wide. Other City players pictured (left to right) Phil Babb and Terry Fleming. A young Alan Shearer is in the background.

October 1992. Amazingly Norwich are top of the table and Coventry second when the two clubs met at Highfield Road. Peter Ndlovu's stunning dribble and goal earns the Sky Blues a 1-1 draw. Here, Andy Pearce heads for goal.

December 1992. In October with the good start petering out, Gould introduced well-travelled striker Mick Quinn. Quinn's impact was the stuff of fantasy. He scored ten goals in his first six games including two goals in the 5-1 win over Liverpool. Here his header sails past Mike Hooper for the fifth.

A week after the Liverpool thriller Quinn does it again, scoring two more in the 3-0 humbling of Villa on Boxing Day. His arrival also rejuvenated his striking partner Robert Rosario (pictured here watching Quinn volley home his first goal).

Phil Babb was signed by Gould for £500,000 from Bradford City in the summer of 1992 and became a regular at left-back. The following season, after the departure of Andy Pearce, he moved to the centre of defence and was a spectacular success. Within a few months he was called into the Republic of Ireland squad and became a star in the 1994 World Cup. When Liverpool offered a British record fee for a defender of £3.75 million it was impossible for City to turn it down.

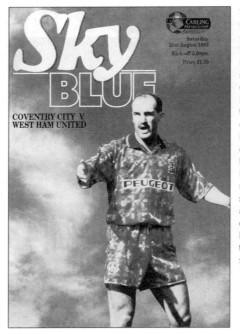

The club went through another financial crisis in the early 1990s and chairman John Poynton was ousted in 1991 to be replaced by Peter Robins, son of Derrick. By the summer of 1993 however Bryan Richardson had emerged as the club's first realistic chairman and one whose business acumen was essential for the new era that football was entering. A new East Stand was built, new roofs installed on other stands, and a new marketing approach to boost the club's off-field income. He was not to blame for the garish shirts that the team played in from 1992-94.

September 1994. Gould's successor Phil Neal took the club to a creditable 11th place in the Premiership but the following season relegation clouds were looming early in the season. Leeds United were beaten with the help of a goal from new signing Dion Dublin. Here Noel Whelan, who joined City just over a year later, takes on Willie Boland and David Busst.

Peter Ndlovu joined City in the summer of 1991 from Highlanders of Zimbabwe. He got his first-team chance within weeks and made an instant impact with his dazzling ball-skills, speed and shooting ability. Between 1991 and 1997 he made almost 200 appearances and scored 41 goals, many of them spectacular. With 26 caps for his country he became the club's most capped player. Here he takes on Sheffield Wednesday's Dan Petrescu in City's 2-0 win in April 1995.

Darren Huckerby was a Newcastle reserve
player when he became Gordon Strachan's first
signing on becoming City's manager in
November 1996. He was an immediate success
with his speed and strength and his
breathtaking goals. He scored three hat-tricks in
less than twelve months, including one at
Elland Road which prompted Leeds to pay £5.5
million to but him in August 1999.

Dion Dublin, signed for £2 million in 1994, was
the club's main source of goals during his four-
year stay at the club, scoring 72 goals in 171
games. A strong and determined striker, Dublin
also shone when asked to play as a centre-back.
Dion became the club's first England international
for over ten years when selected in early 1998.

Soon after Ron Atkinson took over from Phil Neal in February 1995 he appointed Gordon Strachan as his assistant. Although reluctant to play at the age of 38 he helped keep City up in three successive seasons. He became manager in November 1996 and quickly earned a reputation for being outspoken and passionate. His touchline antics and disagreements with referees got him into trouble on numerous occasions. He did, however, keep the Sky Blues in the Premier League and in 1997-98 they finished in the heady position of 11th with an FA Cup semi-final place denied in a penalty shoot-out.

Swedish goalkeeper Magnus Hedman took over from veteran Steve Ogrizovic during the 1997-98 season although Oggie returned for the odd appearance up until April 2000, finally reaching the 600-game mark for the club. The agile Hedman proved an excellent successor with outstanding shot-stopping skills. As the first-choice Swedish keeper he was set to become the club's most capped player during 2001.

During the summer of 1999 the Sky Blues were active in the transfer market. George Boateng moved to Aston Villa for £4.5 million and Huckerby went to Leeds for £5.5 million. In came two Moroccans, Moustapha Hadji (above), African footballer of the year in 1998, and Youssef Chippo. After taking a short time to adapt, Hadji thrilled the fans with his ball-skills and shooting ability.

Hadji, at £4 million, was City's record signing but only held the record for a matter of weeks when City splashed £6 million on Wolves' teenage striker Robbie Keane. Keane scored twice on his debut against Derby and was Carling's player of the month within weeks of arriving. His overall form, plus twelve goals in 34 games, attracted the interest of Internazionale of Milan and in August 2000 he joined the Italian club for £13 million.

The 1999-2000 squad pictured at Ryton. Back row (left to right): S Collie (physiotherapist), D Burrows, Gavin Strachan, M Konjic, M Hyldegaard, M Hedman, R Nuzzo, G Breen, B Ferguson, P Telfer, T Peake (reserve-team coach). MIddle row: G Pendrey (coach), J Aloisi, R Normann, L Delorge, M Hall, P Williams, R Shaw, B Quinn, S Froggatt, M Edworthy, J Blyth (coach). Front row: J Eustace, N Whelan, R Keane, Gordon Strrachan (manager), G McAllister, Y Chippo, M Hadji. The summer of 2000 not only saw the departure of Robie Keane, but also of Gary McAllister, David Burrows and Noel Whelan.

Part of the proceeds of Keane's sale was spent quickly with the £6.5 million purchase of Norwich City's Welsh international Craig Bellamy. He scored two goals in his first three games and whilst not quite in the Keane class, hopes were high that he would become a top class striker in the Premiership. His penalty at the Dell helped City to end a run of 22 away games without a win.

LIST OF SUBSCRIBERS AND VOTES FOR THE MOST POPULAR SKY BLUE

Andy Acton		Moustapha Hadji	Mr Donald W Chalk	George Hudson
Rob Ainsbury			Tony Chattaway	Tommy Hutchison
Mr David M Allen	Bill Glazier	Geoff Clee	Bill Glazier
Phil Amphlett	Lloyd McGrath	Michael Collins	Ernie Machin
Mr Colin Anderson	Tommy Hutchison	John Conway	Dave Bennett
Harry Armstrong	Willie Carr	Paul Cox	Tommy Hutchison
Phil Aston	Tommy Hutchison	William Coyle	Keith Houchen
Dr Graeme Baldwin	Ian Gibson	Colin Craig	87 FA Cup team
Margaret & Terry Barnett	Stewart Robson	Paul Craig	Tommy Hutchison
Joan Barratt	Harry Barratt	A J Cumberlidge	Steve Ogrizovic
Paul Barton	Bill Glazier	Mr Robert Cumberlidge	Tommy Hutchison
Paul Beaman	Ian Wallace	Allan Cunningham	Tommy Hutchison
Clive Beevers	Robbie Keane	Mr R J Daniels	
Mr Garry Anthony Bench	Steve Ogrizovic	Mr Brian Davies	George Hudson
Paul Bennett	Steve Ogrizovic	Edna Davies	Tommy Hutchison
Rick Bennett	Brian Borrows	Andrew Dawes	Cyrille Regis
Marion Bidgood	Roland Nilsson	Roger Dawes	Roland Nilsson
Mike Biggs	Ian Gibson	Rod Dean	Clarrie Bourton
Lionel Bird	Tommy Hutchison	David Delia	David Speedie
Clive Black	Bill Glazier	Mick Devine	Tommy Hutchison
Connor Black	Robbie Keane	Kev Dowling	Steve Ogrizovic
Joshua Black	Colin Hendry	Laura Dumbleton	Robbie Keane
Maeve Black	Trevor Peake	Jeff Earl	Mick Quinn
Jesper Boss	Terry Gibson	Russell Eley	Kevin Gallacher
David Brassington	George Hudson	Mr S G Evetts	George Lowrie
Daniel Brown	Michael Gynn	Eric Howard Eyden	Tommy Hutchison
Jon Brown	Dion Dublin	David Foley	Tommy Hutchison
Sam Brown	Steve Ogrizovic	Michael Ford	Moustapha Hadji
Mark Browne	Tommy Hutchison	Mr F H Fox	Mick Ferguson
Mr Tony Buckingham	Tommy Hutchison	Louise Gallemore	Tommy Hutchison
Mr R Bullard	George Curtis	Robert Gaskins	Ernie Hunt
Paul Bullock	Tommy Hutchison	Ray Gee	George Curtis
Paul Bullock	Steve Ogrizovic	Mark Georgevic	Kyle Lightbourne
Frankie Burke	Tommy Hutchison	Polly Goerres	Peter Ndlovu
Jon Byrne	Trond Soltvedt	Norman Gould	Dennis Mortimer
Barry Carr	Alf Wood	Matthew Gray	Robbie Keane
Keith (Troub) Causer	Tommy Hutchison	Luke Gynn	Michael Gynn

Lewis Handy	**Cyrille Regis**	Mark Lealan	**Kevin Gallacher**
Mick Harrington	**George Curtis**	Phil Lee	**Brian Kilcline**
Malvina Hawkins	**George Curtis**	Mr John Leekey	**Tommy Hutchison**
Colin Heys	**Tommy Hutchison**	Alan Limb	**Steve Ogrizovic**
George Hicks	**George Curtis**	Jonathan Ling	**Cyrille Regis**
Peter R Hindmarch	**Willie Humphries**	Jacob Lloyd	**Robbie Keane**
Gary Hoffman	**Tommy Hutchison**	Dave Long	**Tommy Hutchison**
Martin Hoffman	**Lloyd McGrath**	Peter Louch	**George Curtis**
Paul Hoffman	**Tommy Hutchison**	Selina Marks	**John Eustace**
Simon & Sam Holt	**Steve Ogrizovic**	Craig Marston	**Keith Houchen**
Stephen Holt	**Steve Ogrizovic**	John P Martin	**George Curtis**
Mr W Honour	**Alf Wood**	Michael Hans May	**Steve Ogrizovic**
Stephen Leslie Houghton	**Steve Ogrizovic**	Mr Mike McCarthy	**George Hudson**
Mr Paul Robert Howard	**Tommy Hutchison**	Andrew McElroy	**Dion Dublin**
Roger Hulbert	**Tommy Hutchison**	Trefor McElroy	**Ian Gibson**
Barry Ireland	**Ian Gibson**	James Gordon McEwan	**Brian Borrows**
R A Jacques	**George Hudson**	Geraldine McIlwaine	**Steve Ogrizovic**
Steve James	**Cyrille Regis**	Paul McKay	**David Speedie**
Peter Jardine	**Tommy Hutchison**	Rod Metcalf	**Maurice Setters**
Matt Jessup	**Tommy Hutchison**	Dennis Millman	**George Curtis**
Terje Johansen	**Tommy Hutchison**	A J Moore	**All from 1921**
Phil Johnson	**Mick Ferguson**	Geoffrey Moore	
Dave Jones	**Tommy Hutchison**	Robin Morden	**Steve Ogrizovic**
Gary Jones	**Robbie Keane**	Peter Moseley	**Tommy Hutchison**
Hugh William Jones	**Robbie Keane**	Stephen Mound	**Ernie Machin**
Mr K Jones	**George Curtis**	Antony Mumford	**Tommy Hutchison**
Robert Judd	**George Mason**	Alan Murphy	**Keith Houchen**
J S Keatley	**Willie Carr**	Alan Mynard	**Steve Ogrizovic**
Patrick Kelly	**George Curtis**	Robert Nelsen	**Steve Ogrizovic**
James Kemp	**Steve Ogrizovic**	Graham Nicholls	**Tommy Hutchison**
Spencer Keogh	**Keith Houchen**	Martin Noble	**Tommy Hutchison**
Julie King	**Gary McAllister**	Ben Nunn	**Brian Kilcline**
Len King	**Trevor Peake**	Rune Nyland	**Tommy Hutchison**
Stephen Kingswell	**George Curtis**	Mick Oakes	**Colin Stein**
Mr Christopher Lamb	**Tommy Hutchison**	Robin Ogleby	**Bill Glazier**
Keith Lamb	**Terry Yorath**	John Oughton	**George Curtis**
Chris Lambert	**Tommy Hutchison**	Alex Owen	**John Eustace**
Cheryl Lane	**Cyrille Regis**	Charlie Owen	**Youssef Chippo**
Miss A Lang	**Steve Ogrizovic**	David Owen	**Cyrille Regis**

Eddie Owen	**Moustapha Hadji**	Gary Taylor	**Ernie Hunt**
Graham G Paine	**Steve Ogrizovic**	Gwynne Taylor	**George Lowrie**
David Malcolm Parsons	**Tommy Hutchison**	Martin Taylor	**Ian Wallace**
Sonny Patnaik	**Cyrille Regis**	Michael Tedder	**Tommy Hutchison**
Richard J Peel	**Tommy Hutchison**	Martin Thompson	**Gary McAllister**
David Phillips	**Tommy Hutchison**	Mitch Timms	**Ernie Hunt**
Terry Potts	**Tommy Hutchison**	Chris Tims	**Ian Wallace**
Mr Neil Prestidge	**Terry Yorath**	Richard Tomlins	**Cyrille Regis**
Peter J Race	**George Mason**	John Twigger	**Ian Gibson**
Keith & Angela Reay	**Tommy Hutchison**	Kieran & Aidan Twomey	**Robbie Keane**
Daryl Richardson	**Gordon Strachan**	Phil Walker	**George Curtis**
Mr Simon A Richardson	**Jim Blyth**	David Walters	**Cyrille Regis**
Paul, Patricia & Catherine Roberts	**Robbie Keane**	Adam Ward	**Magnus Hedman**
Stefan Christopher Robey	**Keith Houchen**	Tim Ward	**Steve Hunt**
Chris Russell	**Cyrille Regis**	Mr Robert E Weeks	**Tommy Hutchison**
Sean Ryan	**Tommy Hutchison**	Chris Weir	**Steve Ogrizovic**
R M Sanders	**George Curtis**	Roy West	**George Hudson**
Les Seabourn	**Tommy Hutchison**	Keith White	**George Hudson**
Mr R S Shankland	**Steve Ogrizovic**	Benjamin Willson	**Cyrille Regis**
Leon Shanley	**Lloyd McGrath**	Len & Beryl Wilson	**George Hudson**
Jot Shirley	**Steve Ogrizovic**	Luke & Holly Wilson	**Youssef Chippo**
John Sills	**George Hudson**	Roger & Gill Wilson	**Steve Ogrizovic**
David Simmons	**Tommy Hutchison**	Ian Winham	**Trevor Peake**
Dennis Simpson	**George Mason**	M P Winterton	**Steve Ogrizovic**
Kevin Simpson	**Steve Ogrizovic**	P J Winterton	**George Curtis**
Paul Singleton-Jones	**David Speedie**	Bert Woodfield	**Clarrie Bourton**
Andy Skinner	**Robbie Keane**	Mr John Woodfield	**George Hudson**
Christine Skinner	**Youssef Chippo**	Rich Woodfield	**Ernie Hunt**
Aubery Smith	**Ian Wallace**	Rob Worton	**Tommy Hutchison**
Joe Smith	**Moustapha Hadji**	Bruce Young	**Clarrie Bourton**
Merv Smith	**Ian Gibson**	Mike Young	**George Hudson**
Simon Smith	**Brian Borrows**		
M G Sollis	**George Curtis**		
Mr Christopher Spencer	**George Hudson**		
Kathleen Stewart	**Brian Borrows**		
Marshall Stewart	**Noel Simpson**		
Jonathan Strange	**Cyrille Regis**		
Norman J Styles	**Steve Ogrizovic**		
Neil Sutton	**Steve Ogrizovic**		

MOST POPULAR COVENTRY CITY PLAYER
52 different players received votes

1	**Tommy Hutchison**
2	**Steve Ogrizovic**
3	**George Curtis**
4	**Cyrille Regis**
5	**George Hudson**
6	**Robbie Keane**